What people are say

"Here at Citibank we use the Quick Cou
for 'just-in-time' job aids—the books are great for users who are too busy for tutorials and training. Quick Course® books provide very clear instruction and easy reference."

Bill Moreno, Development Manager
Citibank
San Francisco, CA

"At Geometric Results, much of our work is PC related and we need training tools that can quickly and effectively improve the PC skills of our people. Early this year we began using your materials in our internal PC training curriculum and the results have been outstanding. Both participants and instructors like the books and the measured learning outcomes have been very favorable."

Roger Hill, Instructional Systems Designer
Geometric Results Incorporated
Southfield, MI

"The concise and well-organized text features numbered instructions, screen shots, useful quick reference pointers, and tips…[This] affordable text is very helpful for educators who wish to build proficiency."

Computer Literacy column
Curriculum Administrator Magazine
Stamford, CT

"I have purchased five other books on this subject that I've probably paid more than $60 for, and your [Quick Course®] book taught me more than those five books combined!"

Emory Majors
Searcy, AR

"I would like you to know how much I enjoy the Quick Course® books I have received from you. The directions are clear and easy to follow with attention paid to every detail of the particular lesson."

Betty Weinkauf, Retired Senior
Mission, TX

QUICK COURSE®

in

MICROSOFT®

OUTLOOK® 2000

ONLINE PRESS INC.

Microsoft® Press

PUBLISHED BY
Microsoft Press
A Division of Microsoft Corporation
One Microsoft Way
Redmond, WA 98052-6399

Library of Congress Cataloging-in-Publication Data

Quick Course in Microsoft Outlook 2000 / Online Press Inc.
p. cm.
Includes index.
ISBN 1-57231-991-7
1. Microsoft Outlook. 2. Time management - - Computer programs.
3. Personal information management - - Computer programs. I. Online
Press Inc.
HD69.T54Q53 1999
005.369 - - dc21 98-48185
CIP

Printed and bound in the United States of America.

2 3 4 5 6 7 8 9 QMQM 4 3 2 1 0 9

Distributed in Canada by Penguin Books Canada Limited.

A CIP catalogue record for this book is available from the British Library.

Microsoft Press books are available through booksellers and distributors worldwide. For further information about international editions, contact your local Microsoft Corporation office or contact Microsoft Press International directly at fax (425) 936-7329. Visit our Web site at mspress.microsoft.com.

A Quick Course® Education/Training Edition for this title is published by Online Training Solutions, Inc. (OTSI). For information about supplementary workbooks, contact OTSI at 15442 Bel-Red Road, Redmond, WA 98052, USA, 1-800-854-3344. E-mail: quickcourse@otsiweb.com.

Authors: Joyce Cox and Christina Dudley
Acquisitions Editor: Susanne M. Forderer
Project Editor: Anne Taussig

From the publisher

Quick Course®... The name says it all.

In today's busy world, everyone seems to be looking for easier methods, faster solutions, and shortcuts to success. That's why we decided to publish the Quick Course® series.

Why Choose A Quick Course®?

When all the computer books claim to be fast, easy, and complete, how can you be sure you're getting exactly the one that will do the job for you? You can depend on Quick Course® books because they give you:

- Everything you need to do useful work, in two easy-to-tackle parts: "Learning the Basics" (for beginning users) and "Building Proficiency" (for intermediate users).
- Easy-to-follow numbered instructions and thorough explanations.
- To-the-point directions for creating professional-looking documents that can be recycled and customized with your own data.
- Numerous screen shots to help you follow along when you're not at the computer.
- Handy pointers to key terms and tasks for quick lookup and review.
- Consistent quality—the same team of people creates them all. If you like one, you'll like the others!

We at Microsoft Press are proud of our reputation for producing quality products that meet the needs of our readers. We are confident that this Quick Course® book will live up to your expectations.

Jim

Jim Brown,
Publisher

Content overview

1 Introducing Outlook 2000 — 2

We introduce Outlook and give you an overview of its components. Then we show you how to use Notes to jot down reminders, while demonstrating some of Outlook's organizing techniques. Finally, we show you how to use Help.

2 Managing Contacts — 34

Your contacts list is the heart of your information management system. Here, you add contact information, organize the contact list, and view its information in various ways. Then you customize the contact form to include new information.

3 Communicating with E-Mail — 60

Whether you're working on a stand-alone computer or on a network, this chapter shows you how to use the e-mail component to send, read, and respond to messages. Then you learn ways to organize messages for maximum efficiency.

4 Managing Your Schedule — 84

We show you how to use Outlook's Calendar component to schedule appointments, set up a recurring appointment, and allocate time for longer events. Then you see how to plan meetings and send meeting requests to attendees.

5 Keeping a To-Do List — 108

By using Outlook's Tasks component, you can keep track of tasks and projects in an electronic to-do list. In this chapter, we show how to manage and prioritize onetime and recurring tasks, as well as how to delegate them to other people.

6 Checking Ahead and Looking Back — 124

You fire up Outlook Today to see an overview of the things you need to do today. Then you explore the Journal component, adding specific Outlook activities and documents to its log. Finally, you learn how to archive old Outlook items.

Index — 142

Content details

1 Introducing Outlook 2000 2
What Is Outlook? 4
Getting Started 6
The Outlook Window 7
Creating Notes 13
Editing and Organizing Notes 14
Moving Notes 16
Moving a Note to the Desktop 16
Moving a Note to a Different Outlook Component 17
Deleting Notes 18
Switching Views 19
Creating Your Own View 21
Customizing the Outlook Window 25
Increasing the Size of the Workspace 26
Customizing the Outlook Bar 27
Getting Help 30
Quitting Outlook 33

2 Managing Contacts 34
Adding Contacts 37
Editing and Adding Information 39
Deleting Contacts 41
Organizing Contacts 42
Creating New Categories 43
Switching Views 43
Creating a Custom View 45
Creating Your Own Contact Form 47
Moving Controls and Labels 50
Sizing Controls and Labels 51
Saving a New Form 52
Filling In Custom Forms 53
Using Contacts to Write a Letter 55

3 Communicating with E-Mail 60
Using the Inbox 63
Composing Messages 64
Addressing Messages Quickly 67

Attaching Files to Messages 68
Sending and Retrieving Messages 69
Replying to Messages 72
Forwarding Messages 73
Deleting Messages 74
Organizing Messages 75
Switching Views 76
Applying Custom Filters 77
Using Folders 78
Moving Messages 80
Organizing Messages with the Rules Wizard 80

4 Managing Your Schedule 84
Scheduling Appointments 87
Scheduling Recurring Appointments 90
Scheduling Events 91
Editing Appointments 93
Editing Recurring Appointments 95
Canceling Appointments 95
Finding Appointments 96
Planning a Meeting 98
Sending Meeting Requests 98
Editing Meeting Requests 101
Responding to Meeting Requests 102
Customizing Calendar 103

5 Keeping a To-Do List 108
Adding Tasks 110
Adding Recurring Tasks 114
Editing Tasks 114
Designating Tasks as Complete 115
Deleting Completed Tasks 116
Organizing Tasks 117
Delegating Tasks 120
Dealing with a Task Request 122

6 Checking Ahead and Looking Back 124
Using Outlook Today 126
Making Outlook Today the Starting Component 127
Using Journal 128
Creating Journal Entries 130
Adding an Outlook Item 130
Adding a Contact Activity 132
Adding a Document 134
Opening Documents from Journal 135
Customizing Journal 136
Archiving Outlook Files 138

1

Introducing Outlook 2000

We introduce Outlook and give you an overview of its components. Then we show you how to use Notes to jot down reminders, while demonstrating some of Outlook's organizing techniques. Finally, we show you how to use Help.

In this chapter, you use Outlook to create both business and personal reminder notes to demonstrate that this powerful tool can be used in the office, at school, and at home.

Tasks performed and concepts covered:

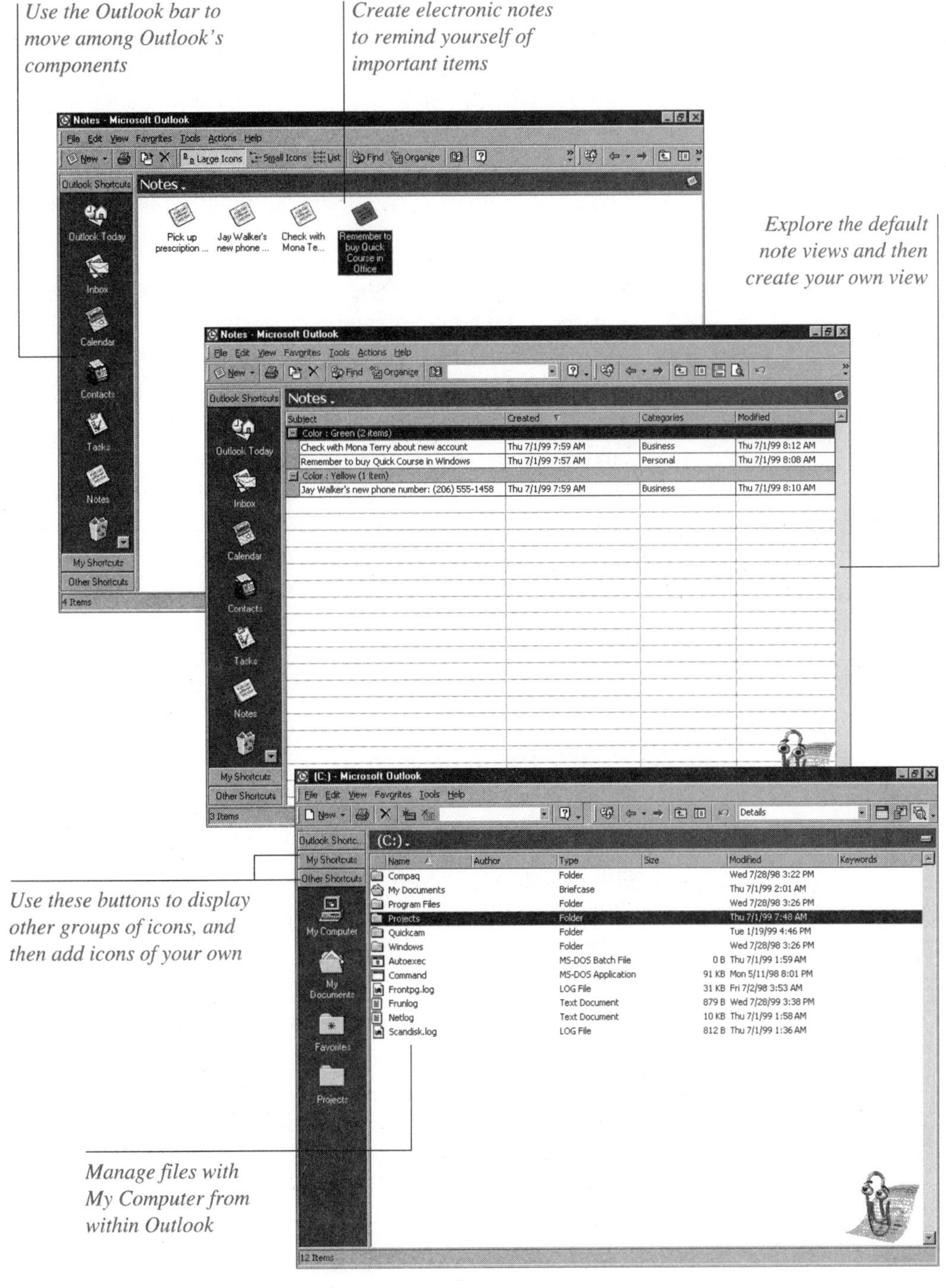

Until recently, it was not uncommon for people to keep track of their appointments, tasks, and other information either in their heads or on various pieces of paper. It's not surprising that things were forgotten or notes were lost, because pieces of paper could easily get buried under paperwork on a desk or could accidentally be moved to the recycling bin. More organized people maintained their information in day-planners, expense recorders, and address books, and either carried several small books around with them or kept everything in a hefty all-in-one organizer.

With the integration of the computer into everyday life, both at work and at home, storing vital business and personal information electronically is a natural step. Although information-management software has been around for some time, in the past programs may have handled some types of information but not others, or may have done a poor job of sharing the information with other programs. Microsoft Outlook 2000 is designed not only as a one-stop information repository but also as a tool for integrating common information-management tasks with productivity programs such as Microsoft Word and Microsoft Excel. This latest version of Outlook thus continues the trend of earlier versions toward tight integration and cross-program accessibility of business and personal information.

What Is Outlook?

You use Outlook to manage the information that you might record in an assortment of address books, appointment books, and notebooks, as well as to handle e-mail. Outlook includes the following components, all of which can be easily customized to fit your needs or preferred methods of organization:

Outlook components

- **Outlook Today.** Provides a handy overview of what's on your plate today. Included are appointments from your calendar, tasks from your to-do list, and the status of your e-mail Inbox, Drafts, and Outbox folders.
- **Inbox.** Keeps track of all your e-mail (and electronic faxes). If you are working on a network, you can communicate with

coworkers via your company's e-mail system; and if you have an Internet account, any Internet e-mail you receive will also show up in your Inbox.

- **Calendar.** Records appointments, including those that occur on a regular basis such as once a month. By default, Calendar reminds you of an upcoming appointment. If you are working on a network that uses Microsoft Exchange Server, you can also schedule meetings with coworkers.
- **Contacts.** Functions as an address book but can store much more information. You can categorize your contacts and store them in different folders, view information in a variety of formats, and track your activites with a particular contact.
- **Tasks.** Maintains a to-do list. You can set Tasks to display reminders or sound alarms to keep yourself on track, and you can schedule time in Calendar for working on to-do list items.
- **Journal.** Can automatically record computer activities, such as working on a document or sending an e-mail message. You can also create manual journal entries to track phone calls and other types of information.
- **Notes.** Creates reminders that replace hand-written notes. You can leave the reminders open on the desktop, organize them from within the Notes component, or move the information they contain to another Outlook component.

In this chapter, we discuss some Outlook basics by introducing you to the Notes component. You will get to know the Outlook window, learn how to create notes, and see how to customize your view of the window's contents. Many of the techniques we demonstrate with Notes also apply to the other Outlook components, which we'll discuss in the remaining chapters. In this book, we focus on Outlook's most useful features—the ones most people will use most often and the ones more people would use if they knew how. By the time you finish this Quick Course book, you'll have a firm understanding of the components of Outlook, and you'll know enough to experiment on your own with the features we don't cover in detail.

Getting Started

We assume that Outlook has been installed on your computer either separately or as part of the Microsoft Office 2000 package. We also assume that you have experience working with Microsoft Windows (95, 98, or NT 4 or later). If you are new to Windows, we recommend you take a look at the appropriate edition of *Quick Course®* in Microsoft Windows, which will help you quickly come up to speed.

Let's take a look at Outlook now. Follow these steps:

The Microsoft Outlook icon

1. On the Windows desktop, double-click the Microsoft Outlook icon to start the program.
2. If Outlook is not yet configured for your computer, the Outlook 2000 Startup Wizard appears to set it up. Complete the wizard's dialog boxes and rejoin us when you've finished.
3. If necessary, click the Office Assistant's Start Using Microsoft Outlook option. (We discuss the Office Assistant on page 30. As you work through this chapter, the Office Assistant will entertain you with some cute antics and may display a

Corporate support vs. Internet support mode

Some features of Outlook are available only if you are working on a network that runs Microsoft Exchange Server. When Outlook was installed, the setup program detected whether your computer was connected to a network and whether it had a modem, and configured Outlook for corporate support on networked computers or Internet support on stand-alone computers. If the setup program couldn't determine how you are going to use Outlook, a dialog box or two may request clarification when you start the program.

Automatic Outlook start-up

To start Outlook when you turn on your computer, add an Outlook shortcut to your StartUp folder. Right-click a blank area of the taskbar and choose Properties from the shortcut menu. In the Taskbar Properties dialog box, click the Start Menu Programs tab, and click Add to start the Create Shortcut Wizard. Click Browse and navigate to the C:\ Program Files\Microsoft Office\ Office folder, double-click Outlook, and click Next. Select the StartUp subfolder, click Next, and click Finish. Then click OK.

Changing the default starting component

If you use a different Outlook component more often than the Inbox, you can specify that Outlook display that component's window when the program starts. Choose Options from the Tools menu, and on the Other tab, click Advanced Options in the General section. Click the arrow to the right of the Startup In This Folder edit box, select the desired component, and click OK twice. The next time you start Outlook, it will open with the window of the component you selected displayed in the workspace.

message or a light bulb. Other than responding to messages by clicking an option, you can ignore it for now.)

4. Maximize the Outlook window, which should look something like the one shown here:

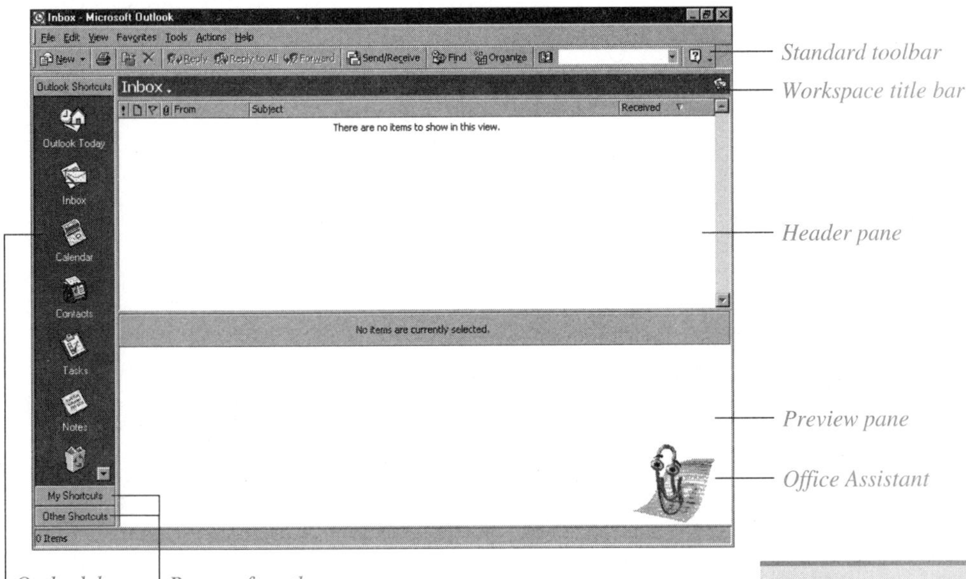

By default, Outlook opens with the Inbox component displayed. We currently have no messages, but you might see a welcoming message from the Outlook development team. If your computer is set up to automatically log onto your e-mail server, you may see other new and existing e-mail messages. (We discuss e-mail in more detail in Chapter 3.)

The Outlook Window

Like the windows of most Windows applications, the Microsoft Outlook window includes the familiar title bar at the top and a status bar at the bottom. You can also see the menu bar and Standard toolbar at the top of the window and a shortcut bar down the left side. Although the menu bar and toolbar look similar to those in all Windows applications, they work a little differently, so we'll take a moment to explain them here. Then we'll look at the shortcut bar.

Different configurations

We wrote this book using a computer running Windows 98 with a screen resolution of 800x600. If you are using a different version of Windows or a different resolution, the appearance of your screens won't match ours exactly. We also used the Outlook configuration that results when you do a Typical installation of Microsoft Office 2000 from CD-ROM on a networked computer. If your setup is different, don't worry. You will still be able to follow along with most of the examples in this book. Finally, we have hidden the Windows taskbar by right-clicking it, choosing Properties, selecting AutoHide, and then clicking OK.

The *menu bar* provides access to commands for working with Outlook. The Outlook menus work the same as those of other Windows applications, except that Outlook ranks the commands on each menu. First it determines which ones you are most likely to use and hides the others, and then as you work with the program, it adjusts the display of commands on each menu to reflect the tasks you perform. As a quick example, let's take a look at the View menu:

Choosing commands

1. Click *View* on the menu bar to drop down the View menu. The two arrows at the bottom of the menu indicate that one or more commands are hidden because they are not the ones most people use most of the time.

Personalized menus and toolbars

Outlook's menus and toolbars adjust themselves to the way you work, making more commands and buttons available as you use them. Commands and buttons you don't use are hidden so that they don't get in the way. As a result, your menus and toolbars may not look exactly like ours, and occasionally, we may tell you to choose a command or click a button that is not visible. When this happens, don't panic. Simply pull down the menu and wait for all its commands to be displayed, or click the toolbar's More Buttons button to display its hidden buttons. If you ever want to restore your menus and toolbars to their original settings, simply choose Toolbars and then Customize from the View menu and on the Options tab, click Reset My Usage Data and then click OK. (You can also assign the toolbars to separate rows by deselecting the options in the Personalized Menus And Toolbars section of this tab.)

2. Continue pointing to the word *View*. The two arrows disappear, and more commands appear on the menu, like this:

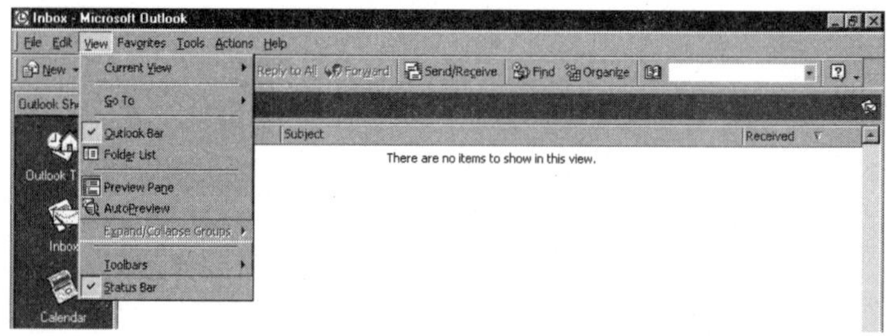

(You can also click the two arrows to make hidden commands appear.) The status of a less frequently used command is indicated by a lighter shade of gray. If you choose one of the light gray commands, in the future it will appear in the same color as other commands and will no longer be hidden.

3. Move the pointer away from the menu bar and the menu and then press Esc twice to deactivate them both.

The *toolbar* is a collection of buttons that provide instant access to common commands. Clicking a button on the toolbar is the equivalent of choosing the corresponding command from a menu and if necessary, clicking OK to accept all the default settings in the command's dialog box. Outlook comes with several built-in toolbars equipped with buttons that help you accomplish specific tasks. Let's display another toolbar so that we can show you how to work with multiple toolbars:

1. Right-click the Standard toolbar to drop down a shortcut menu of the other available toolbars.
2. Choose Advanced from the menu. The Advanced toolbar now spans the top of the workspace, like this:

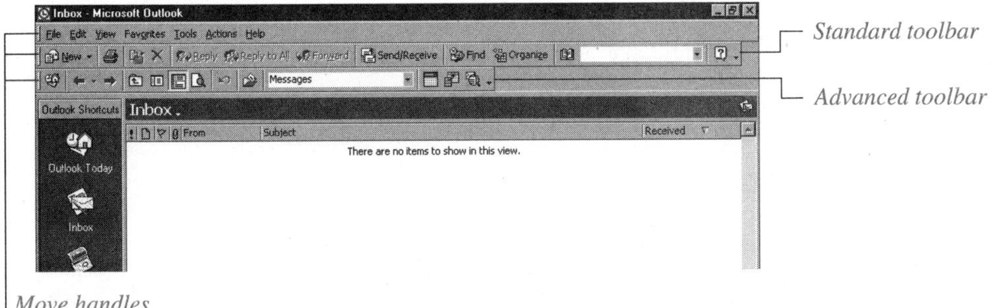

3. Familiarize yourself with the buttons on the Advanced toolbar by pointing to each one in turn. The *ScreenTips* feature displays a box with each button's name.

ScreenTips

4. Point to the Advanced toolbar's *move handle* (the gray bar at the left end). When the pointer changes to a four-headed arrow, drag the toolbar over the workspace. It becomes a "floating" toolbar, like this:

Moving toolbars

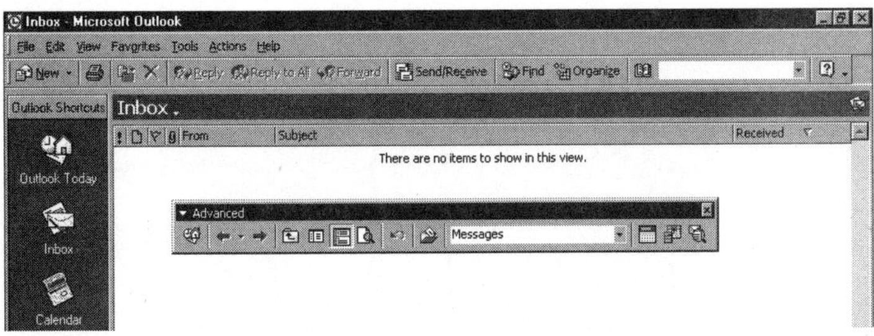

5. Double-click the floating toolbar's title bar to "dock" it back at the top of the workspace.

So far the toolbar has behaved predictably. But now try this:

1. Point to the Advanced toolbar's move handle and drag the toolbar up over the Standard toolbar. The two toolbars arrange themselves on one toolbar row, as shown on the next page.

Docking in other locations

As well as docking a toolbar above the workspace, you can dock it along the bottom or down the sides by simply dragging it to those locations. If you then convert the toolbar to a floating bar, double-clicking its title bar docks the toolbar in its previous location.

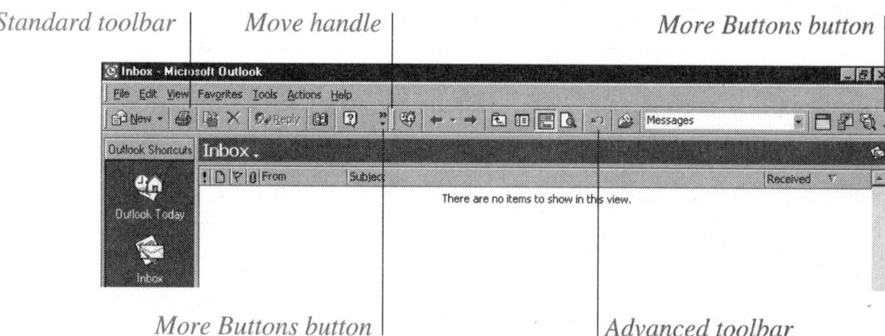

2. Point to the Advanced toolbar's move handle again, and this time drag all the way to the right until only four buttons are visible, as shown here:

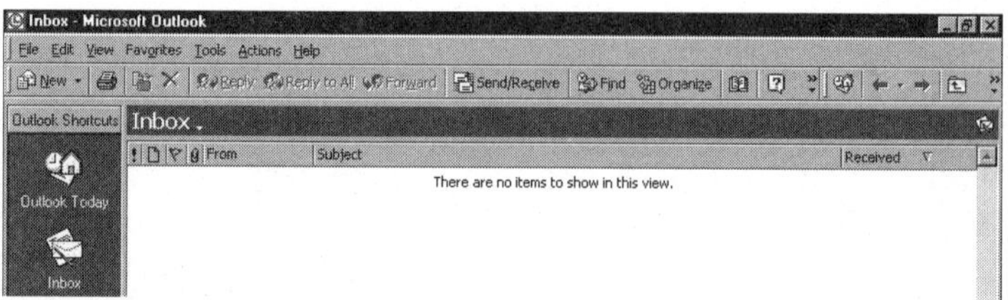

Just as Outlook ranks the commands on menus, it ranks the buttons on the toolbars. When you display less of a toolbar, as you have here, Outlook hides the buttons it thinks you will use less frequently. When you display more of a toolbar, hidden buttons reappear in their usual places.

The More Buttons button

3. Click the Advanced toolbar's More Buttons button to see this palette of all the hidden buttons on that toolbar:

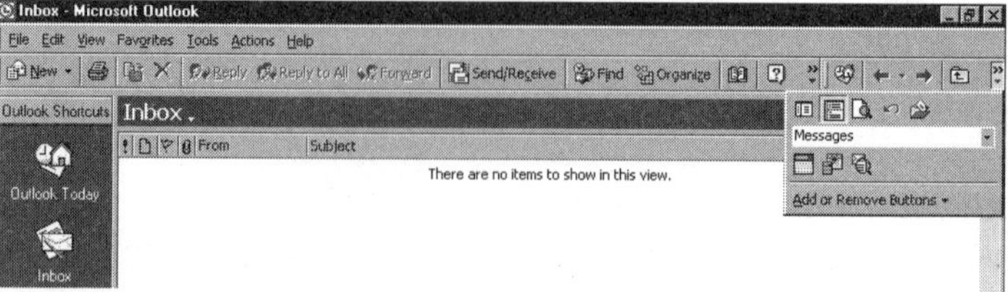

The Folder List button

4. Click the Folder List button. Outlook opens a hierarchical list of its components, and the Folder List button joins the four other buttons on the Advanced toolbar.

5. Now click the Folder List button again to close the list.

6. Click the Standard toolbar's More Buttons button and point to Add Or Remove Buttons. You see this drop-down menu:

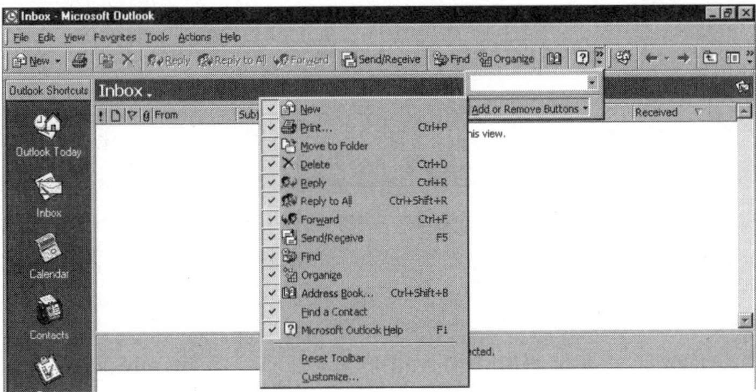

If you know you will never use some of these buttons, you can deselect them in the list to remove them from the toolbar. To add them back, all you have to do is select them again.

7. You don't want to make any changes right now, so press Esc three times to close the drop-down menu, close the palette, and deselect the More Buttons button.

8. If you want, experiment some with the toolbars. When you've finished, set them up as shown in the screen above and rejoin us for a look at the shortcut bar.

The pane on the left side of the Outlook window is a versatile navigation tool known as the *Outlook bar*, which you can use to jump quickly from one Outlook component to another, as well as to various locations on your computer or network. By default, the Outlook bar consists of three groups of components, each of which has a button displaying its name. Clicking a button opens its group. The Outlook Shortcuts group is currently open, providing easy access to the Outlook components. Follow these steps to check out the other groups:

1. First click the My Shortcuts button at the bottom of the pane to open that group, which contains the icons for the default e-mail folders, the Journal component, and a link to the Outlook Update page of Microsoft's Web site.

Initial capital letters

Sometimes the capitalization of the option names we use doesn't exactly match what's on the screen. We capitalize the first letter of every word to set them off in a sentence. For example, in the adjacent steps, we tell you to point to Add Or Remove Buttons, when the option on the screen is Add or Remove Buttons.

Switching between small and large icons

2. Right-click the Outlook bar and choose Large Icons from the shortcut menu. Now the icons in this group look the same as those in the Outlook Shortcuts group. (When a group contains more icons than will fit on the bar in large icon view, as the Outlook Shortcuts group does, choose Small Icons so that you can see them all at once, or click the down arrow at the bottom of the bar to bring more icons into view.)

3. Click the Other Shortcuts button to display its group, which contains icons for My Computer and the My Documents and Favorites folders. You can use this group to store shortcuts to other folders to enable you to quickly find files or jump to specific Web sites.

4. Finish up by opening the Outlook Shortcuts group.

The Outlook workspace

The header and preview panes

The area to the right of the Outlook bar, called the *workspace,* displays the contents of the icon selected in the Outlook bar. In the case of the Inbox, the workspace is further divided into a *header pane,* which displays summary information about the messages in your Inbox, and a *preview pane,* which displays the text of the message selected in the header pane. (For more about displaying and reading e-mail messages, see page 69.) Let's see how the Outlook bar and workspace work:

1. Click various icons in the Outlook Shortcuts group to jump from one component to another, and then redisplay Inbox in the workspace.

2. Click the arrow at the bottom of the bar to see the hidden icon.

The Notes icon

3. Now click the Notes icon. The buttons on the Standard toolbar change, and the workspace title bar indicates that the Notes component is now active, like this:

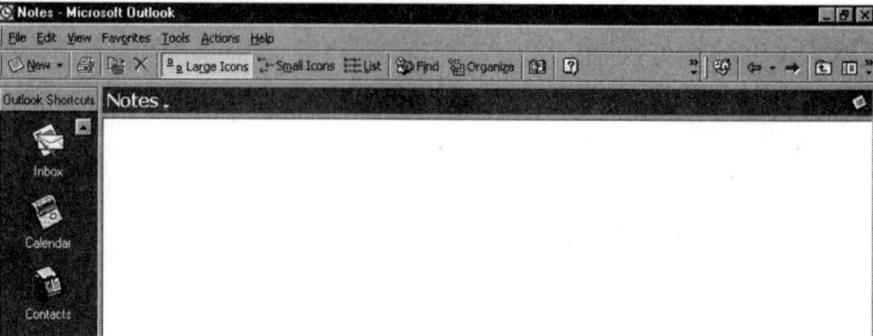

Your Notes workspace may contain a sample note. You can ignore it for now. It won't get in the way, and we'll show you how to delete it later. As we mentioned earlier, you use the Notes component to jot down any tidbits of information you want to keep handy. The main advantage of keeping notes in Outlook instead of on pieces of paper is that you can easily use the information contained in the note with a different Outlook component.

Creating Notes

The best way to see how the Notes component of Outlook works is simply to start creating some notes. Suppose you want to remind yourself to purchase another book in the Quick Course series. Follow these steps:

The New Note button

1. With the Notes window displayed, click the New Note button on the Standard toolbar. Outlook displays a small yellow box, similar to the "sticky" notes used in most offices:

   The note box has an icon in the top left corner that you can click to display a menu of commands related to the note, and a Close button (the X) in the top right corner. At the bottom of the note box is the date and time the note was created.

2. With the insertion point blinking in the blank note box, type *Remember to buy Quick Course in Office.*
3. Outlook automatically saves the note as soon as you close it, so simply click the Close button.
4. Create a few more notes by clicking the New Note button on the Standard toolbar and typing the items listed on the next page. (Be sure to click the Close button when you finish one note and click the New Note button to start a new one.)

Other ways to create notes

To create a note while you are working in another Outlook component, simply click the arrow to the right of the New button on the Standard toolbar and select Note, or choose New and then Note from the File menu.

Check with Mona Terry about new account

Jay Walker's new phone number: (206) 555-1458

Pick up prescription at drug store

5. When you finish the last note, click its Close button. Your notes are now displayed in the workspace like this:

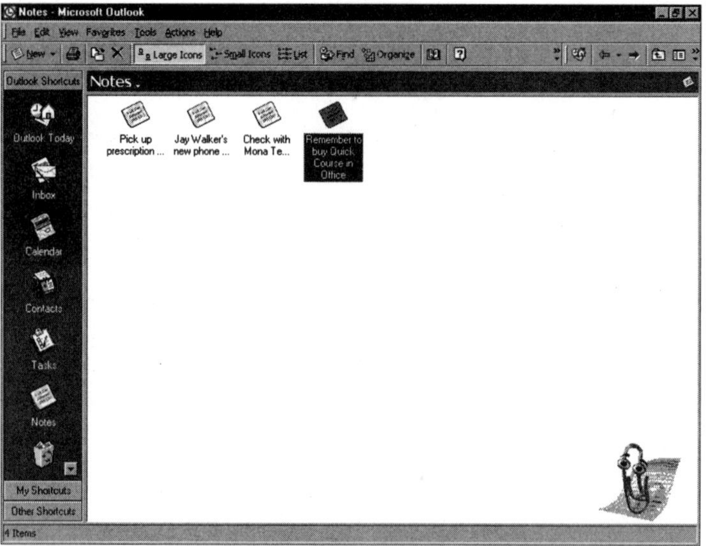

Notes displays the entire text of the selected note and the first few words of all the others. To select a note, simply click it.

Saving notes

Because notes are constantly saved, you can open a note, make a change, and then click the Close button to save the change. If you want to save a note for use in another program, open the note, click the icon in the top left corner, choose Save As from the menu, and assign a name and storage location as you would with any other file. By default, Outlook saves the note as a Rich Text Format (RTF) file. To select a different format, click the arrow to the right of the Save As Type box and then make your selection.

Editing and Organizing Notes

Suppose you want to edit a note you have created. Or suppose you want to change its color to make it stand out, or organize the notes into categories. Let's experiment:

1. Double-click the book reminder, select the word *Office*, and type *Windows*.
2. Change the color of the note from yellow to green by clicking the icon in the top left corner of the note box and choosing Color and then Green from the menu.

Assigning a note to a category

3. You don't want this personal note to get buried among your business-related notes, so click the icon again and choose Categories from the Notes menu to display the dialog box shown here:

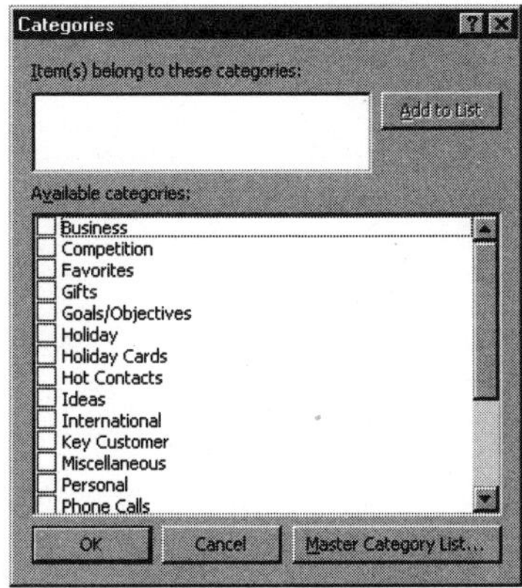

4. Click the Personal check box in the Available Categories list and click OK. Although nothing appears to happen, Notes now stores this note in the personal category, as you will see when we discuss different ways of viewing notes on page 19.

5. Save and close the note by clicking its Close button.

6. Double-click the Mona Terry note, repeat steps 3 and 4 to assign the note to the business category, change its color to green to indicate that it's important, and close the note.

7. Double-click the prescription note, assign it to the personal category, and close it.

8. Now double-click the Jay Walker note and assign it to the business category, but don't close the note box.

9. Move the mouse pointer to the bottom right corner of the box, and, when the pointer changes to a double-headed arrow, hold down the mouse button and drag diagonally toward the top left corner. Release the mouse button when the box is just big enough to display its text, as shown at the top of the following page.

Changing note defaults

To change the Notes default color, choose Options from the Tools menu and on the Preferences tab, click the Note Options button. Change the note color by clicking the arrow to the right of the Color box and making a selection. You can change the default note-box size by clicking the arrow to the right of the Size box and making a selection. To change the default font for notes, click the Font button to display the Font dialog box, make your changes, and then click OK. To implement your changes, click OK twice.

The note box remains this size unless you change it again.

10. Click the note's Close button to save your changes and to close the box.

Moving Notes

You may be wondering why the Notes feature is so great if you can't see the notes when you move to another Outlook component or to a different application. Fortunately, you can move your notes onto the desktop and display them there no matter what application you are working with. You can also move the contents of the note to another Outlook component.

Moving a Note to the Desktop

Suppose the Mona Terry note is so important that you want to be able to see it while you work on other things, just so you won't forget it. Follow these steps to make the note accessible even if Outlook is not running:

1. With Notes displayed on your screen, double-click the Mona Terry note to open it in its box.
2. Resize the box so that it is just large enough to display its text.
3. Minimize Outlook by clicking the Minimize button at the right end of the title bar. The active note now appears on the desktop, as shown here:

Minimizing Outlook

4. If necessary, move the note box to a blank area of the screen by pointing to its title bar, holding down the left mouse button, and dragging to the desired location. When the box is where you want it, release the mouse button.

Minimizing a note

5. Now double-click the My Computer icon and maximize the My Computer window. The note seems to disappear, but it has actually been minimized on the taskbar.

Displaying a note's text

6. If necessary, point to the bottom of your screen to display the taskbar, and then point to the Check With Mona Terry button on the taskbar. Windows displays a pop-up box containing the text of the note, as shown here:

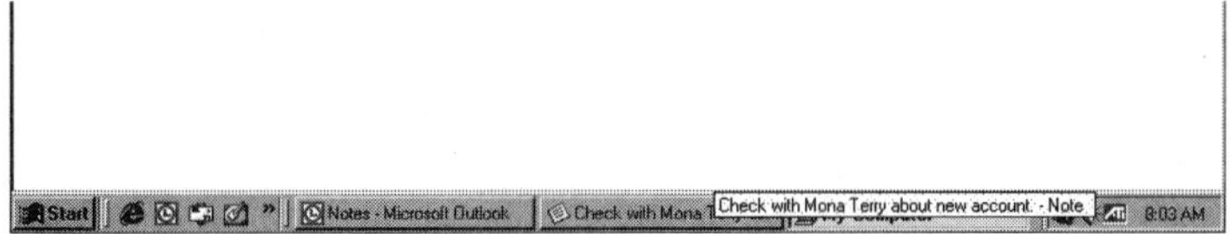

If the note were longer, only the first several words would be displayed.

Displaying a note box

7. To display the note box, simply click the button on the taskbar. An insertion point is blinking in the note box, ready for you to make any changes.

8. Click the note's Close button and close My Computer.

9. Then click the Notes button on the taskbar to redisplay the Outlook window.

Moving a Note to a Different Outlook Component

If you want to move the text of a note to another Outlook component, you simply select the note in the Notes workspace and drag it to the appropriate Outlook component icon. For example, suppose you want to convert the prescription note into a task on your to-do list. Follow these steps:

1. Click the prescription note once to select it, point to it, hold down the left mouse button, and drag the note to the Tasks icon on the Outlook bar.

2. When the shadowed box attached to the pointer is positioned over the Tasks icon, release the mouse button. Outlook displays this window, with the text of the note displayed in the Subject edit box:

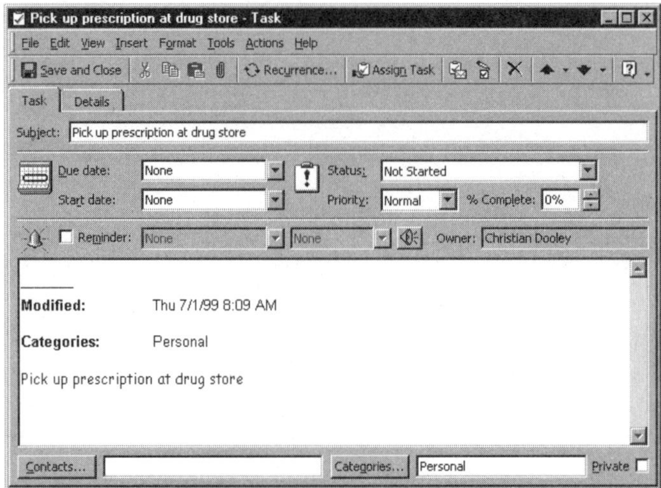

3. We discuss the Tasks component in greater detail later in Chapter 5. For now, simply click the window's Close button and then click No when asked whether you want to save the changes you have made.

As you read the remaining chapters of this book, bear in mind that you can easily move the contents of a note to another Outlook component to get you started in creating a new contact, appointment, or e-mail message. Very handy!

Attaching a note to another Outlook item

Sometimes you may want a note to appear as an attachment inside another Outlook item. For example, you might want to write the instructions for getting to a business conference as a note and then attach the instructions to an appointment in your calendar. To attach a note to an item in another Outlook component, open the component and the item and then choose Item from the Insert menu. In the Insert Item dialog box, click the Notes folder to display its contents and then select the appropriate note from the Items list at the bottom of the dialog box. Check that the Attachment option is selected in the Insert As section and then click OK. Now the note is embedded in the item. To open the note, simply double-click it.

Deleting Notes

When a note is no longer useful, you will want to delete it to keep it from hogging space in the Notes workspace and on your hard drive. Delete the prescription note now by following these steps:

1. If necessary, click the prescription note once to select it.

The Delete button

2. Click the Delete button on the Standard toolbar. The note instantly disappears.

3. Repeat steps 1 and 2 to delete any notes you don't want, being sure to keep the three other notes you have created in this chapter.

4. Suppose you decide you don't want to delete the last note after all. You haven't made any other editing changes, so choose Undo Delete from the Edit menu to redisplay this note.

5. Choose Redo Delete from the Edit menu to delete the note once again.

Switching Views

One of the main benefits of Outlook is that the program is easily customizable to your needs. Let's explore some of the ways you can view notes, bearing in mind that you can also view items in the other Outlook components in similar ways:

1. Click first the Small Icons button and then the List button on the toolbar to see what those icon views look like.

2. Click the Large Icons button to redisplay the original view.

Suppose none of these icon views quite fits the bill. Let's look at some of the table views Outlook has to offer:

1. Choose Current View and then Notes List from the View menu to display the notes in the table view shown below:

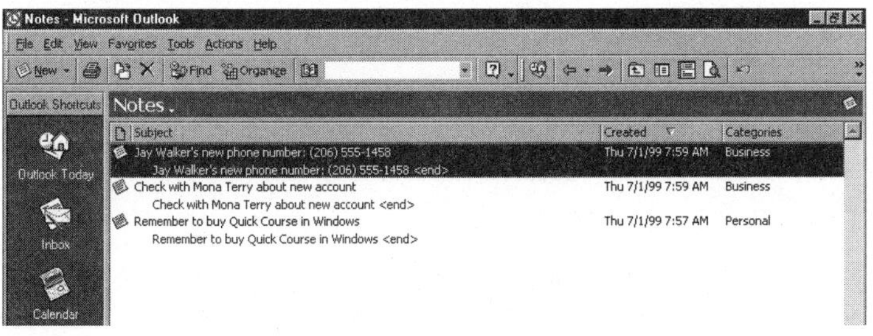

As you can see, Outlook displays information about the notes in Icon, Subject, Created, and Categories fields. The Icon field displays a note icon of the appropriate color, and

Retrieving deleted items

If you decide later that you want to retrieve a note (or another Outlook item), you can display the contents of the Deleted Items folder by clicking its icon on the Outlook bar. Select the note you want to retrieve and drag it to the Notes icon. Then when you display your Notes in the workspace, the note you retrieved will then be back in its place.

the Subject field displays the first few lines of the note (using an ellipsis if the entire text is too long to fit in the allotted space). The Created field displays the date and time the note was created, and the Categories field displays the category the note is assigned to, if any.

Sizing fields

2. Point to the border between the headers for the Subject and Created fields, and when the mouse pointer changes to a double-headed arrow, drag to the left. Release the mouse button when the Subject field is just wide enough to display the text of the three notes. (Notice that the Created and Categories fields expand so that you can read more of their information.)

3. Choose Current View and then By Category from the View menu. Notes now looks like this:

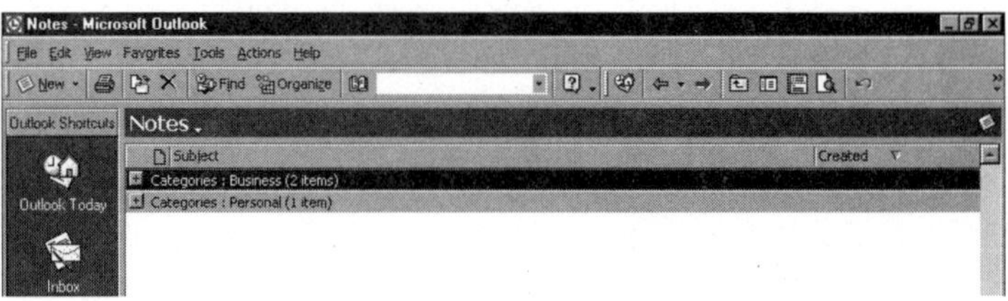

The notes are now grouped by the categories to which you assigned them.

Expanding categories

4. To display the notes in a particular category, click the category's plus sign. For example, Notes appears like this after you expand both categories:

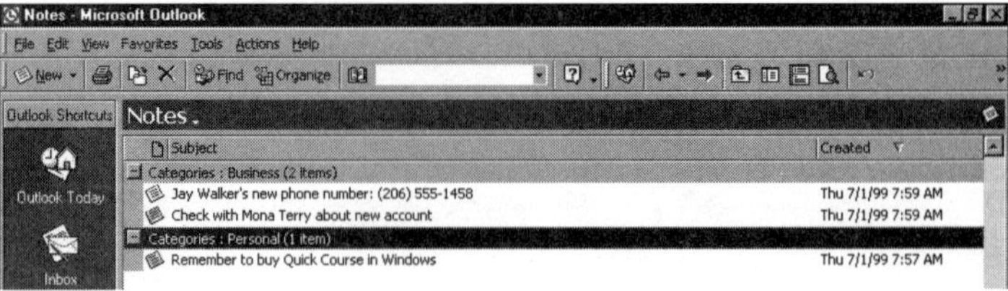

Contracting categories

5. To collapse the categories again, simply click each category's minus sign.

6. Now choose By Color from the Current View submenu to display a window in which the notes are grouped by color.

7. Finally, choose Last Seven Days from the Current View submenu to display only notes created in the last seven days. (In this case, all three notes were created within the last seven days, so this option looks similar to notes list view.)

Creating Your Own View

Suppose none of Outlook's views organizes your notes exactly the way you want them. You don't have to settle for the closest match because, with Outlook, you can create your own view. Here's how to modify an existing view to create one that better suits you:

1. Switch to the by color view and expand the color categories to display the notes.

2. Choose Current View and then Customize Current View from the View menu to display the dialog box shown here:

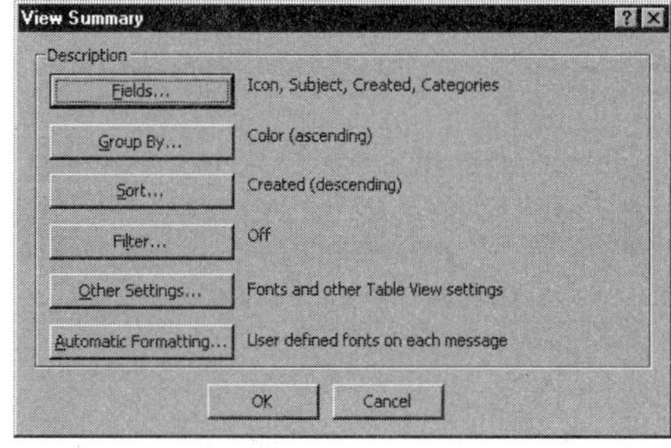

3. Click the Group By button to display this dialog box:

Sorting (grouping) notes

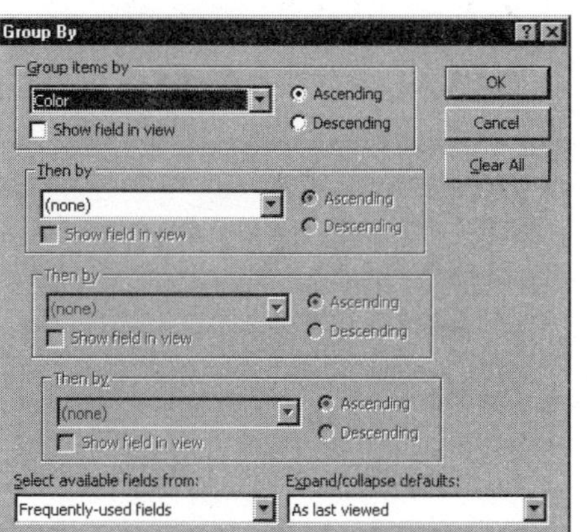

You can select up to four grouping levels for your notes. By default, the Group Items By edit box uses the selected view as the first grouping level (in this case, Color). You can then select either Ascending (A to Z or lowest to highest digit) or Descending (Z to A or highest to lowest digit) to determine how that group should be sorted.

4. For this example, leave the default Ascending option in the Group Items By section selected.
5. Click the arrow to the right of the first Then By edit box and select Categories. Check that the Ascending option next to the edit box is selected and then click OK in both dialog boxes. Outlook sorts the notes first by color and then by category within each color.
6. Click the plus sign next to each color category.
7. Next click the plus sign next to each Categories subcategory to display the details of each note, as shown here:

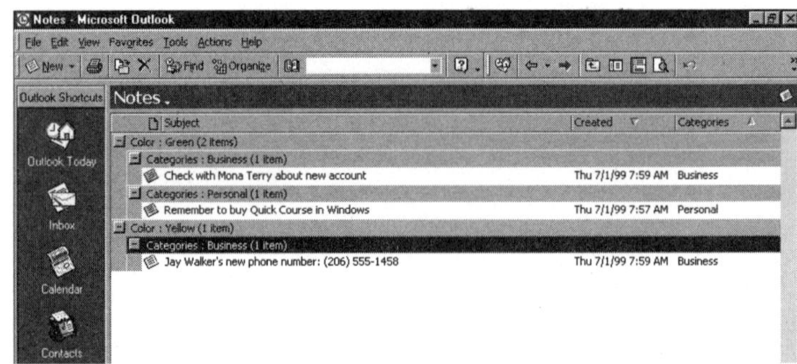

8. Repeat steps 2 and 3 to open the Group By dialog box again, select (None) from the first Then By edit box, and click OK twice to redisplay the notes sorted by color only.

For an even more flexible way of changing views or creating new ones, you can use the Define Views dialog box. Try this:

1. Choose Current View and then Define Views from the View menu to display the dialog box shown at the top of the facing page.

Grouping items

To quickly group items in any table view, you can use the Group By box. When you right-click a field header in a table view and choose the Group By Box command from the shortcut menu, Outlook displays the box above the table in the workspace. To group by a particular field, drag the field's header to the Group By box. Outlook instantly sorts the items in the table by that field and removes the field's information from the table. To group by more than one field using the Group By box, drag another field's header to the box and release the mouse button when the red double-headed arrow appears to the right of the first field header. If you want this new field to be the first group-by field, drag the field header to the left of the current first field. To fine-tune any grouping, double-click an empty area of the box to display the Group By dialog box. To remove a grouping field entirely, drag the field header anywhere outside the Group By box and then release the mouse button when Outlook shows a large black X over the column heading. To return a field header and its information to the table, drag the field header over to the table's header row, releasing the header when it is positioned where you want it. To close the Group By box, right-click a field header in the table and choose Group By Box from the shortcut menu.

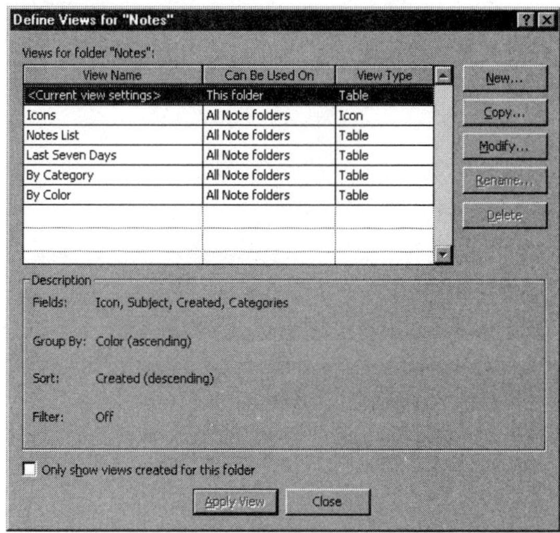

At the top of the dialog box, Outlook displays a list of the available views (in this case, the current view and the five default Notes views). Information about the view selected in the list appears in the Description section. You can create a new view from scratch by clicking the New button, copy a view (which you can then rename and modify in order to create a new view) by clicking the Copy button, or modify an existing view by clicking the Modify button.

2. With Current View Settings selected, click the Copy button to display this dialog box:

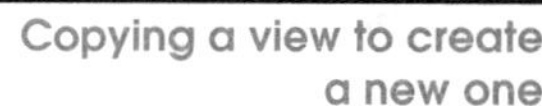

Copying a view to create a new one

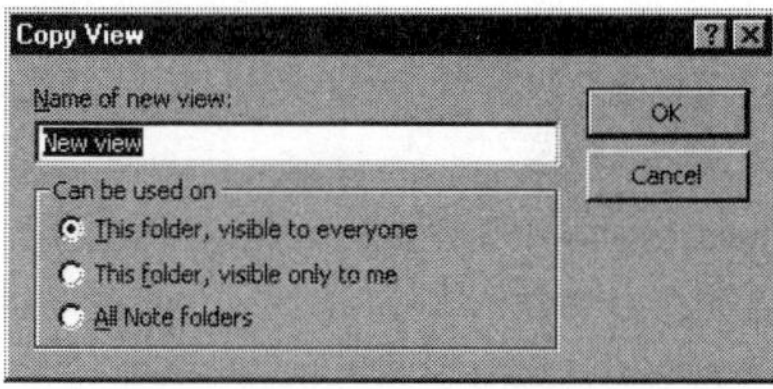

3. Type *My View* in the Name Of New View edit box and then click OK to open the View Summary dialog box we showed earlier on page 21.

4. Next click the Fields button to display the dialog box shown on the next page.

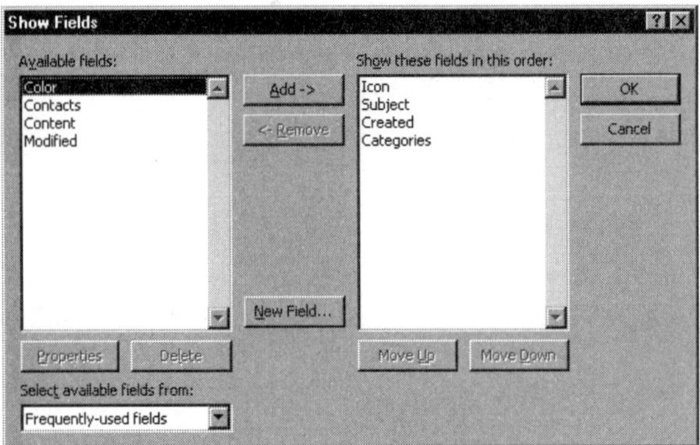

5. The Icon field isn't very useful, so select it in the Show These Fields In This Order box and click the Remove button.

6. Click Modified in the Available Fields box and click the Add button to add a field that records when the note was edited.

Specifying field order

7. To move the Modified field to the bottom of the list, click the Move Down button twice. Then click OK to return to the View Summary dialog box.

Your custom view now has the fields you want, but suppose you'd like to add gridlines to the table. Follow these steps:

Changing the formatting of a custom view

1. Click the Other Settings button to display this dialog box:

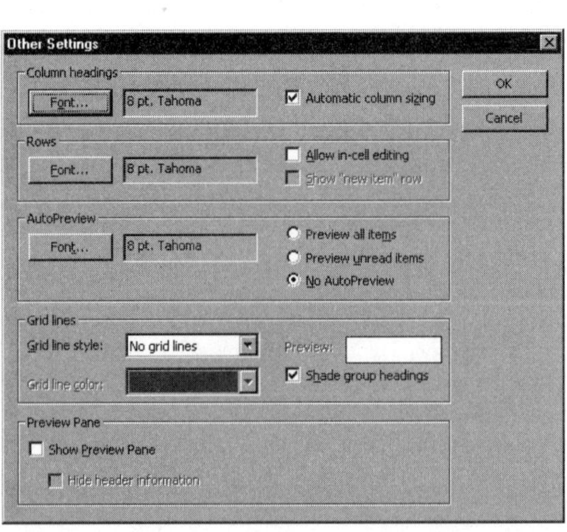

You can use the first few sections of this dialog box to change the font for various parts of the note.

The available fields

In the Show Fields dialog box, the fields that are listed in the Available Fields box are determined by the setting in the Select Available Fields From edit box. You might want to select various options from this drop-down list to see the range of fields that can be added to custom table views.

2. Click the arrow to the right of the Grid Line Style box in the Grid Lines section and select Solid.

3. Click the arrow to the right of the Grid Line Color box and select a color you feel is appropriate. Then click OK twice to close first the Other Settings dialog box and then the View Summary dialog box.

4. Click Close to close the Define Views dialog box and create the new view.

5. Choose Current View and then My View from the View menu and, if necessary, expand the color groups and adjust the column widths. The Notes workspace displays solid colored gridlines between entries, includes a Modified field at the end of the table, and no longer includes an Icon field, as shown here:

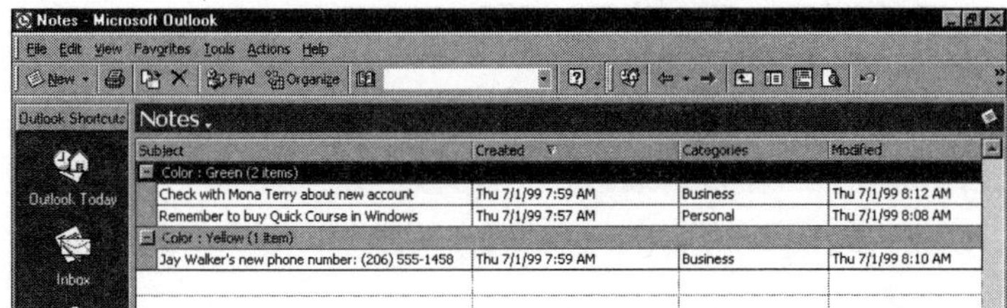

If you no longer need a custom view, just delete it, like this:

Deleting a custom view

1. Switch to the by color view.

2. Choose Current View and then Define Views from the View menu to display the dialog box shown earlier on page 23.

3. Select My View from the Views list and click the Delete button. Click OK when asked to confirm the deletion, and then click Close.

Moving fields manually

To move fields manually in any table view, simply point to the header of the field you want to move, hold down the left mouse button, and drag the header to the desired location. Outlook displays a red arrow to show where the column will move when you release the mouse button. You can move fields this way in any Outlook component.

Customizing the Outlook Window

You can modify parts of the Outlook window to get a better view of your information and to keep your other resources within easy reach. While you are still learning to use Outlook, you may want to stick with the default setup to keep things simple. But as you get more familiar with the program, you might want to experiment with some of the capabilities we'll quickly cover in this section until you find the configuration that best suits the way you work.

Increasing the Size of the Workspace

No matter how you change the view of your information, you may find the workspace is still too small. The simple solution is to reclaim space used by other window elements. Try this:

Turning off the status bar

1. Choose Status Bar from the expanded View menu to turn off the bar at the bottom of the window.

Sizing the Outlook bar

2. Point to the right border of the Outlook bar and drag to the left as far as you can.

Hiding the Outlook bar

3. Now right-click the Outlook bar and choose Hide Outlook Bar from the shortcut menu. Your screen now looks like this:

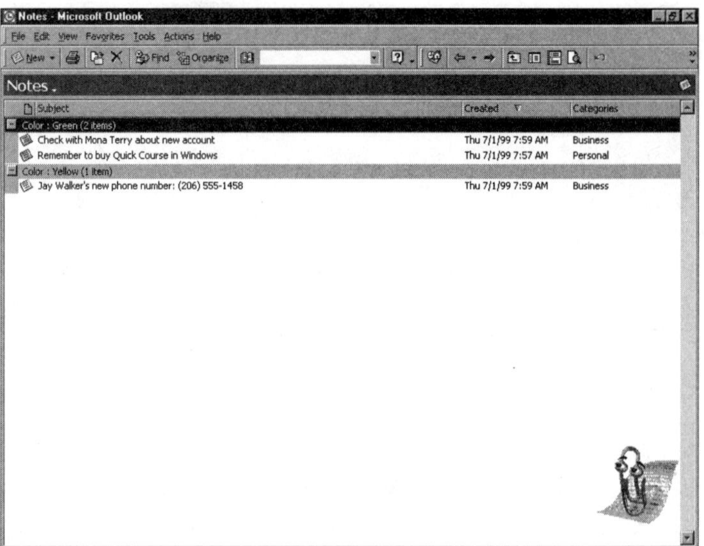

Well, that's all well and good, but now how do you move from one Outlook component to another? Try this:

Moving among Outlook components

1. Click the arrow to the right of the word *Notes* in the workspace title bar to display a list of all available destinations, and click Inbox to display its contents in the expanded workspace.
2. Click the arrow to the right of *Inbox* and then click Notes to redisplay its contents.

3. Click the Notes arrow and then click the push pin in the top right corner of the list box to keep the list open, as shown here:

The Push Pin icon

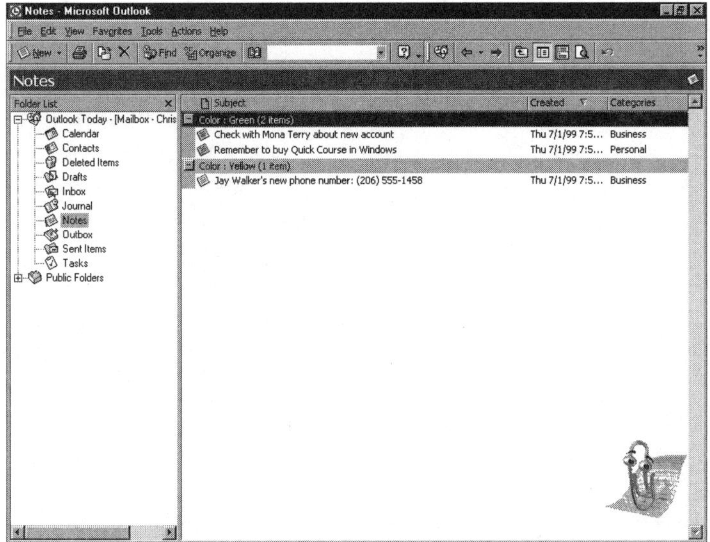

4. To close the folder list, click the Close button at the right end of its title bar, or click the Folder List button on the Advanced toolbar, or choose Folder List from the View menu. (You can also choose this command to display the list.)

5. Choose Outlook Bar from the View menu to turn the bar back on, and restore its original size by dragging its right border to the right. Then redisplay the status bar.

Another way of moving around when you have turned off the Outlook bar is to choose Go To from the View menu and then choose a destination from the submenu. You can move directly to Outlook Today, Inbox, Calendar, Contacts, or Tasks, and you can move to any other destination by choosing Folder to display a dialog box similar to the folder list. You can also initiate various Internet or intranet activities. You might want to check out the Go To submenu on your own before moving on.

The Organize button

You can use the Organize button as another method for organizing Outlook items and changing views. When you click the Organize button on the Standard toolbar, Outlook opens a pane in the top half of the workspace to help streamline the organization process. When the Using Folders option is selected, you can tell Outlook to move selected items to a specific folder or click New Folder to create a new one. When the Using Views option is selected, you can select a different view or customize the current view. To close the Organize pane, either click its Close button or click the Organize button again to toggle it off.

Customizing the Outlook Bar

When you first start working with Outlook, you may think of it as only a personal information and e-mail manager. But Outlook is flexible enough to function as the interface through which you can initiate many of the other tasks you need to perform throughout the day. By adding shortcuts for folders to the Outlook bar, you can quickly open documents without ever having to close Outlook.

In this section, we briefly discuss ways to add these shortcuts and otherwise modify the Outlook bar. For demonstration purposes, suppose you keep all your current work in a Projects folder on your hard drive and you want to keep this folder close at hand so that you can easily open any of its documents. Follow these steps to create the folder:

Creating a new folder

1. Click the Other Shortcuts button to open its group, then click the My Computer icon to show its contents in the workspace.
2. Double-click the icon for your hard drive. Choose New from the File menu and then Folder from the expanded submenu.
3. Type *Projects* as the name of the new folder and press Enter.

Now we'll show you how to add a shortcut for the folder to the Other Shortcuts group:

Adding shortcuts to the Outlook bar

1. Select the Projects folder, drag it into the Other Shortcuts group, and position the black bar below the other icons. The new Projects icon looks like this:

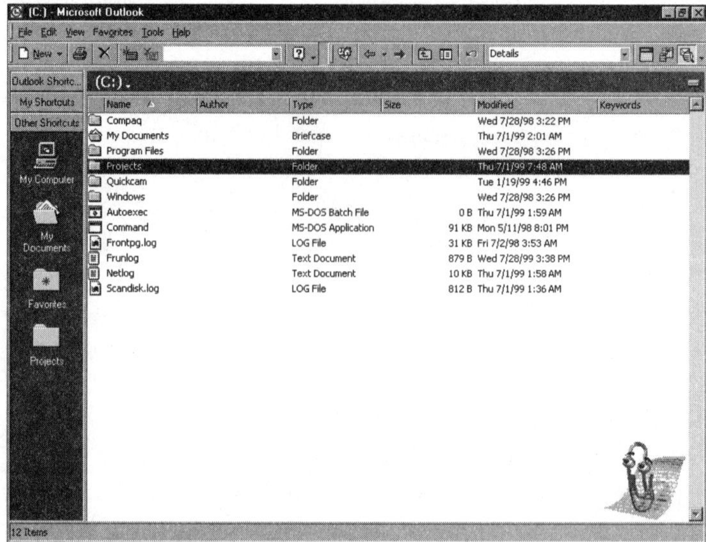

Dragging to another group

To drag folders or files from one group to another, select the item you want to move and then drag it to the appropriate group button on the Outlook bar. Pause until Outlook displays the group's contents in the Outlook bar, move the pointer to the desired location, and release the mouse button. If you drag a folder or file to a different group, Outlook's default action is to move it. You can copy it by holding down the Ctrl key.

To work on a document stored in the Projects folder, you can simply click the Projects icon in the Other Shortcuts group to display its contents in the workspace, and then double-click the document's icon to open it in its application.

Moving shortcuts

2. Because all your current work is in this folder, you want it at the top of the Other Shortcuts group. Point to the Projects folder, hold down the left mouse button, drag the black bar upward, and then release the mouse button when it is above My Computer.

After you have added shortcuts to a particular group, you may want to change the group's name to better reflect its shortcuts. Try this:

Renaming groups

1. Right-click a blank area of the Other Shortcuts group and choose Rename Group from the shortcut menu.
2. With Other Shortcuts highlighted on its button, type *Current Work* and press Enter.

To avoid confusion, you had better reverse your steps here and return the Other Shortcuts group to its original status. Here are the steps:

1. Repeat steps 1 and 2 above, changing the group's name back to *Other Shortcuts*.

Removing shortcuts

2. Right-click the Projects icon on the Outlook bar and choose Remove From Outlook Bar from the shortcut menu, clicking Yes when asked to confirm the deletion.
3. Click the My Computer icon, double-click the icon for your hard drive, right-click the Projects folder, and choose Delete from the shortcut menu to erase the demonstration folder. If necessary, click Yes to confirm the deletion.

Well, that wraps up our discussion of some of the different ways you can modify Outlook's views. But before we end this chapter, we'll take a quick look at how you can get help if you ever get stuck.

Adding and removing groups

To add a group to the Outlook bar, right-click the bar and choose Add New Group from the shortcut menu. Then type the name of the new group and press Enter. To remove a group, right-click its button and choose Remove Group from the shortcut menu. Click Yes to confirm that you want to delete the group.

Getting Help

This tour of Outlook has covered a lot of ground in just a few pages, and you might be wondering how anyone could possibly remember it all. Don't worry. If you forget how to carry out a particular task, help is never far away. You've already seen how the ScreenTips feature can jog your memory about the functions of the toolbar buttons. And you may have noticed that each dialog box has a Help button (the question mark in the top right corner) that provides information about its options. Here, you'll take a look at ways to get information using the Office Assistant. Follow these steps:

The Microsoft Outlook Help button

1. Click the Outlook Shortcuts button, click the Notes icon, and then click the Microsoft Outlook Help button on the toolbar. If you are prompted to install the Help feature, do so. The Office Assistant then displays a message that gives you several options, as shown here:

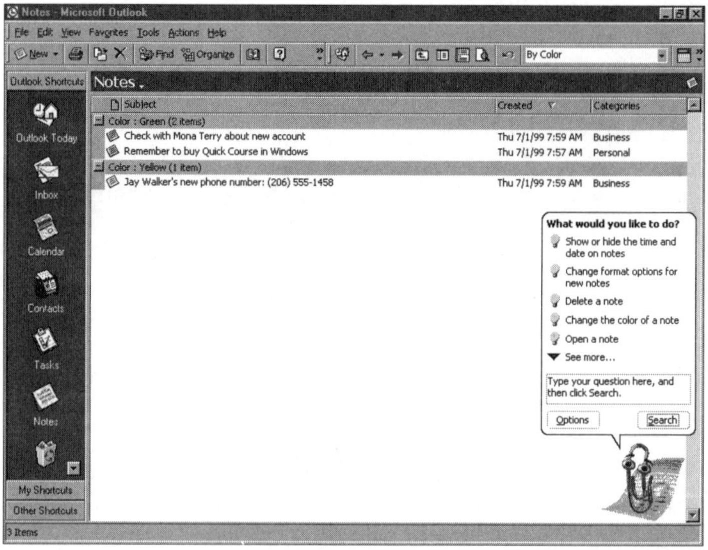

Office Assistant options

If the Office Assistant displays a light bulb above its icon, click the light bulb to see a tip. To move the Office Assistant, simply drag it. To make it temporarily disappear or reappear, choose Hide/Show The Office Assistant from the Help menu. To remove it permanently or customize it, click the Office Assistant's Options button. In the Office Assistant dialog box, select or deselect options that control when the Office Assistant appears, whether it makes sounds, and what tips it displays. On the Gallery tab, you can click the Back or Next buttons to scroll through the characters available for the assistant and click OK to change it. (You may need to insert the installation CD-ROM to complete the switch.)

(If the Office Assistant is already displayed, you can simply click it to see its message.) The Office Assistant's options reflect the work you have been doing. If you don't find any of the current options helpful, you can type a question in the Search box and click the Search button to have the Office Assistant look for topics that most closely match your question.

2. Type *Change views* and click the Search button. The Office Assistant displays a list of related topics.

3. Click the Change The View option to display the Help window shown below. (Outlook may take a few seconds to prepare the Help file.)

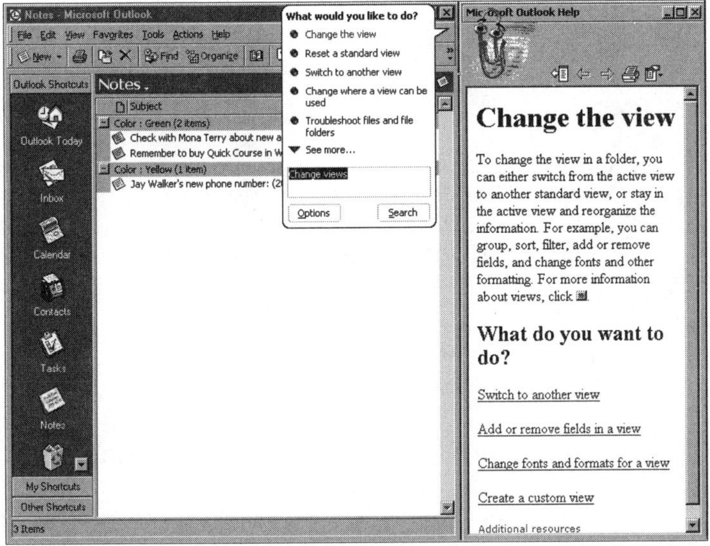

4. Read through the information and then click the Change Fonts And Formats For A View topic to display instructions on how to complete the task.

5. Click the Back button to move back to the Change The View topic and then explore other options.

The Back button

6. Click the Help window's Close button.

Some people prefer to get help by looking through an index of topics. Try that now by following these steps:

1. Choose Microsoft Outlook Help from the Help menu to display the Office Assistant's list of topics, and then click any topic to display the Help window.

2. Click the Show button to expand the Help window, and click the Index tab. Your screen now looks like the one shown on the next page.

The Show button

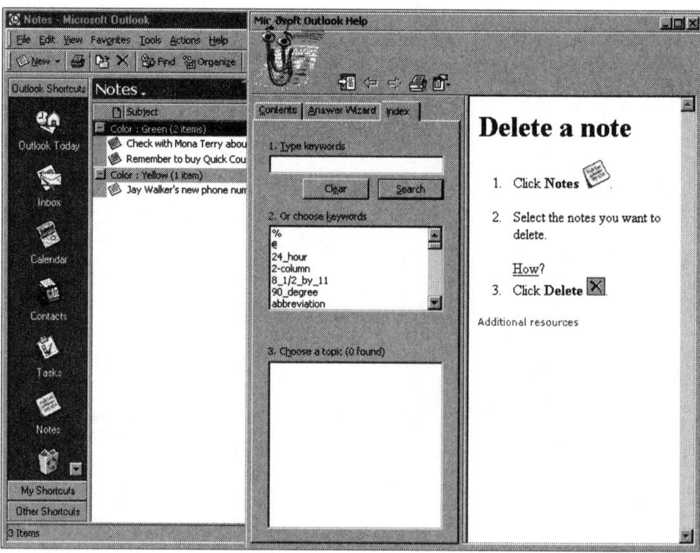

3. In the edit box, type *view*. The list below scrolls to display key words beginning with the letters you type.
4. Click the Search button to display a list of pertinent topics.
5. Next click the Change The View index entry. Help displays the steps necessary for changing the view, as shown on the previous page.
6. Click the Close button.

We'll leave you to explore other Help topics on your own as you need them.

Using Contents

The Contents tab of the Help window displays various topics represented by book icons and their subtopics represented by question mark icons. To display a topic's subtopics, click the plus sign to the left of the book icon. When you find the subtopic you're looking for, click it. Help displays the information in the window on the right of your screen.

Using Answer Wizard

The Answer Wizard provides a way to type search questions when the Office Assistant is turned off. Display the Help window, click the Answer Wizard tab, type a question in the edit box, and then click Search. Outlook displays a list of topics that most closely fit the question. You can then double-click one of the topics to display its contents in the right pane.

Using the Web

If you have a modem and are connected to the Internet, you can access the Microsoft Office Update Web site as well as other Microsoft Web sites to get information or technical support. Choose Office On The Web from the Help menu to start your Web browser, connect to the Internet, and display the Microsoft Office Update Web site.

Quitting Outlook

Well, that's a lot of work for one chapter, and you're probably ready for a break. All that's left is to show you how to end an Outlook session. To take full advantage of Outlook's capabilities to periodically check e-mail, remind you of appointments, and display notes throughout the day, you can start Outlook when you begin your day and then minimize it when it's not in use. (You can also have Outlook automatically start up when you turn on your computer—see the tip on page 6.) Then you quit the program only when you're ready to go home at the end of the day. When you are ready to quit Outlook, here's what you do:

1. Choose Exit from the File menu.

Here are some other ways to quit Outlook:

- Click the Close button at the right end of Outlook's title bar.
- Press Alt, then F (the underlined letter in *File* on the menu bar), then X (the underlined letter in *Exit* on the File menu).
- Double-click the Control menu icon (the envelope/clock icon) at the left end of Outlook's title bar.

2 Managing Contacts

Your contact list is the heart of your information management system. In this chapter, you add contact information, organize the contact list, and view its information in various ways. Then you customize the contact form to include new items of information.

The contact list you create includes only professional acquaintances, but storing contact information electronically can help you work more efficiently at the office, for your community group, or at home.

Tasks performed and concepts covered:

Create a custom form that includes special information fields

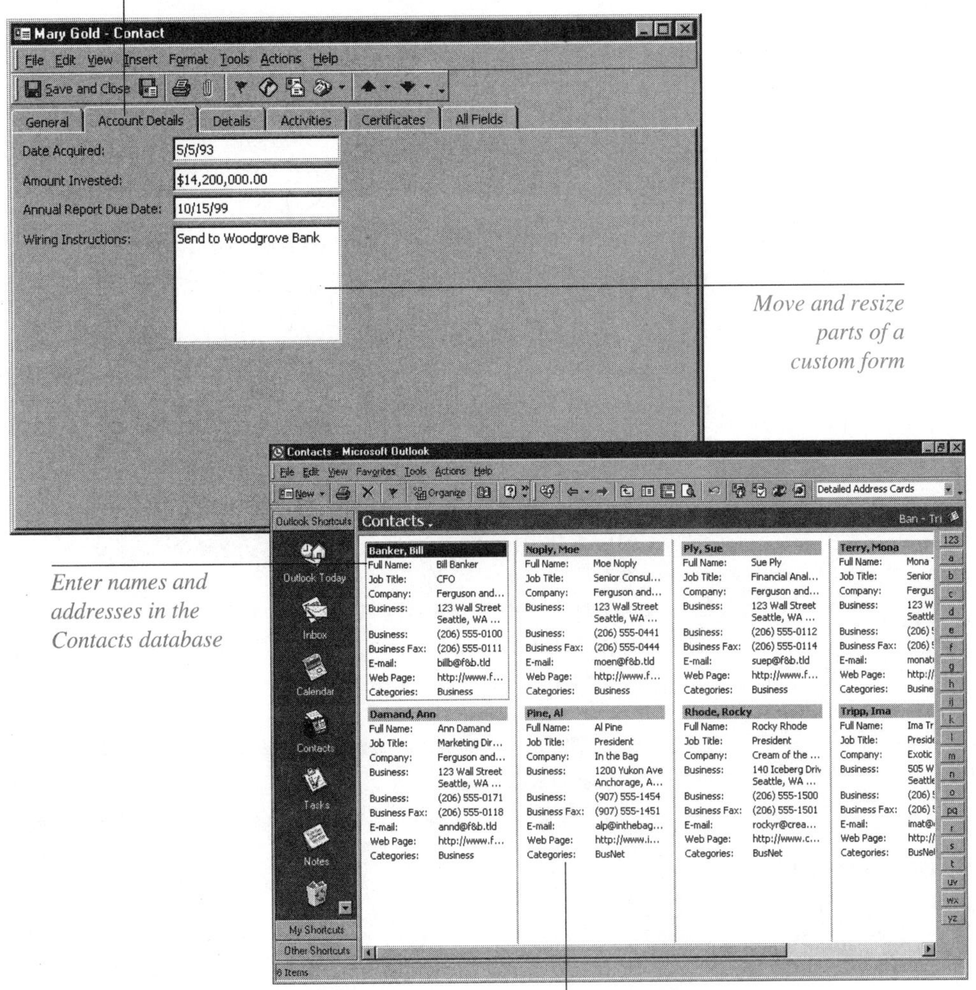

Explore different ways to view the Contacts database

During the work day, you do things that involve other people, such as sending e-mail messages, scheduling meetings, or tracking tasks and projects. You need to store information about the people you frequently interact with in some type of database.

The Contacts component of Outlook performs the tasks of an electronic address book. You can look up addresses when writing letters or sending invoices or reports, and your computer can dial phone numbers for you. But Contacts also stores e-mail and Web page addresses, and it allocates space for additional information about each contact. What's more, Contacts tracks your activities in relation to each of your contacts so that you can easily check what you did and when.

In this chapter, you'll explore many of the features of the Contacts component. As you'll see, developing a contact list when you first start using Outlook helps streamline activities performed in other Outlook components. Let's get started:

The Contacts icon

1. With Outlook open on your screen, click the Contacts icon on the Outlook bar to display its contents in the workspace.
2. If necessary, right-click the toolbar and select Advanced. Then adjust the toolbars so that they each occupy about half the toolbar row. Your screen now looks like this:

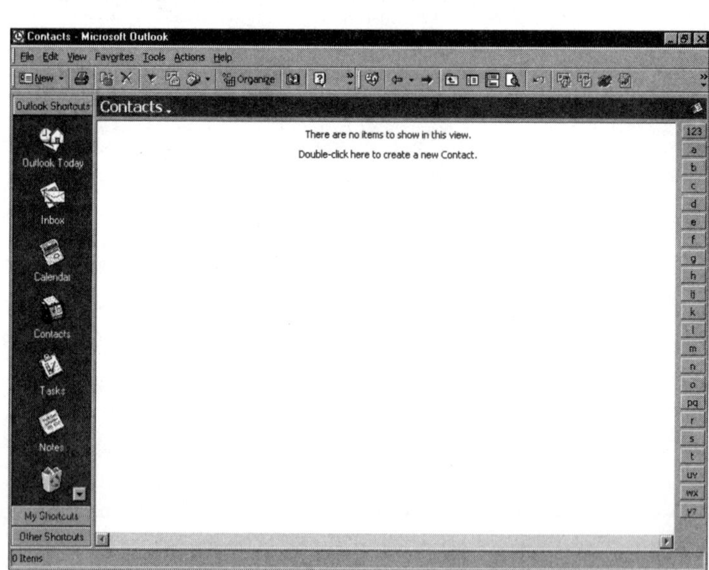

Importing and exporting contacts

If you have created a list of names and addresses in another application, you can import it into Contacts. Choose Import And Export from the File menu, select the desired action in the Import And Export Wizard's first dialog box, and click Next. Then follow the wizard's instructions. To export a list from Contacts to another program, follow the same procedure, selecting the desired export option in the first dialog box.

As you can see, we've hidden the Office Assistant by right-clicking it and choosing Hide. Because you have not used Contacts before, your list is empty except for any entries, called *address cards*, that have been created by Outlook. Down the right side of the workspace are alphabet buttons, like the tabs for pages in a standard address book.

Address cards

Adding Contacts

Creating a contact list is easy. In this section, you build a list for a fictional money management firm called Ferguson and Bardell. Let's add a few address cards to the workspace:

The New Contact button

1. Click the New Contact button on the toolbar to display this Contact window:

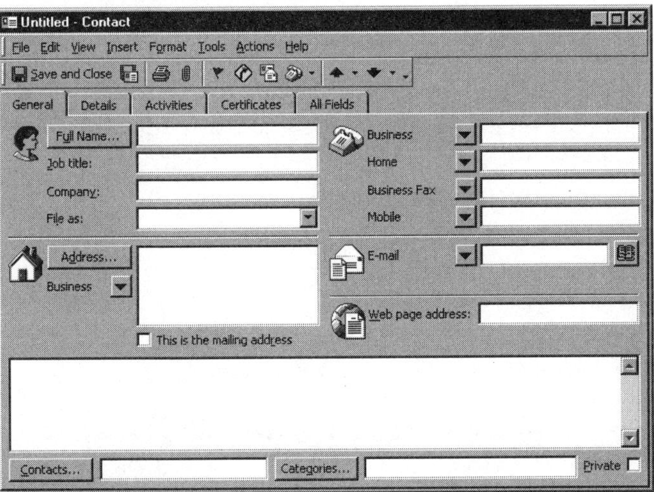

2. In the Full Name edit box, type *Mona Terry* and press tab. (You can click the Full Name button to make sure Outlook has accurately broken down the name into its component parts—first and last names, for example—for use when creating documents such as form letters.) Notice that Outlook has entered *Terry, Mona* in the File As box for sorting purposes. (You can change this entry to *Mona Terry* by clicking the arrow to the right of the box.)

3. In the Job Title edit box, type *Senior Consultant* and press Tab. Then type *Ferguson and Bardell* in the Company edit box.

Other ways to add new contacts

If you are working in another Outlook component and want to quickly add a new contact, you can simply click the arrow to the right of the New button at the left end of the Standard toolbar and select Contact from the drop-down list. You can also choose New and then Contact from the File menu. If you prefer to use keyboard shortcuts, press Ctrl+N to enter a new contact from within the Contacts component or press Ctrl+Shift+C to enter a new contact from another component.

4. Click the arrow to the left of any of the edit boxes in the Phone section and notice that you can reassign the boxes to record the ways you can get in touch with this contact. Press Esc to close the list of possibilities without reassigning any boxes.

5. Enter *2065550222* as the Business number and *2065550223* as the Business Fax number. Outlook inserts the appropriate parentheses and hyphens when you move to a different box.

6. In the Address box, type *123 Wall Street*, press Enter, and type *Seattle, WA 98105*. Then click the Address button to check that the address is correctly broken down into its component parts. (As you can see, this is the business address for this contact. You could click the arrow below the Address button, select Home or Other from the list, and enter another address.) Because you have entered only one address, Outlook assumes this is the contact's mailing address and checks this option.

Entering multiple addresses

7. Enter *monat@f&b.tld* in the E-mail edit box. (You can enter up to three e-mail addresses per contact by clicking the arrow to the left of the edit box and assigning a new type. You can search for e-mail addresses in an existing address book by clicking the Address Book button to the right of the edit box.)

The Address Book button

8. Enter *www.f&b.tld* in the Web Page Address edit box. Outlook converts the address to an active Internet link, and the Contact window should now look like this:

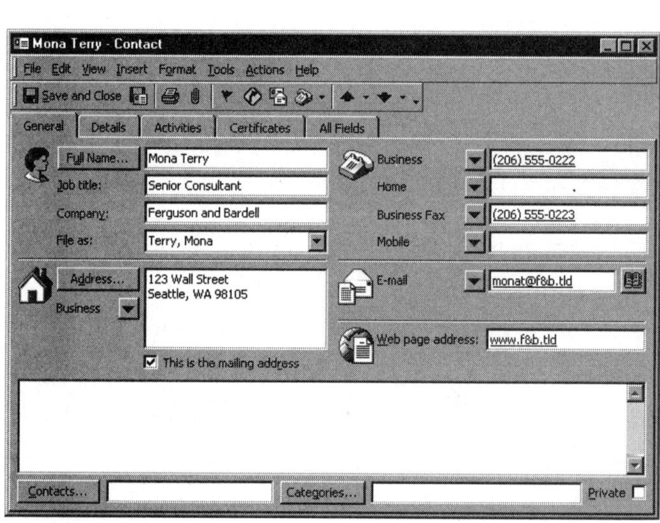

About e-mail addresses

The e-mail addresses you enter for our examples are Internet e-mail addresses. They consist of a user (mailbox) name, followed by the @ sign, followed by a domain name that identifies the mail server. If you enter information for people within your organization, you'll most likely enter only their user names as their e-mail addresses because with internal e-mail, everyone's mailbox is usually stored on the same mail server.

9. To assign Mona Terry to the business category, click the Categories button at the bottom of the Contact window to display the Categories dialog box shown earlier on page 15. Then click the Business check box and click OK.

The Save And New button

10. Click the Save And New button to save the current address card and display a blank Contact window.

11. Create address cards for the people listed below, entering *Ferguson and Bardell* as the company name, *123 Wall Street, Seattle, WA 98105* as the address, and *www.f&b.tld* as the Web address. Assign them all to the business category. Then click the Save And Close button after the last one.

The Save And Close button

Name	*Sue Ply*	*Ann Damand*	*Bill Banker*	*Moe Noply*
Job Title	*Financial Analyst*	*Marketing Director*	*CFO*	*Senior Consultant*
Bus. Phone	*2065550112*	*2065550117*	*2065550100*	*2065550441*
Bus. Fax	*2065550114*	*2065550118*	*2065550111*	*2065550444*
E-mail	*suep@f&b.tld*	*annd@f&b.tld*	*billb@f&b.tld*	*moen@f&b.tld*

Editing and Adding Information

Once you add an address card to your contact list, you can easily edit the information on the card by double-clicking the card in the workspace to redisplay the Contact window. Looking over the address cards now in the workspace, suppose you discover an error in the Ann Damand card. Here's how to edit existing contact information:

Displaying an address card

1. Double-click *Damand, Ann* to display her address card.

2. Change *0117* in the phone number to *0171* and click Save And Close.

Underlined entries

In the Contact window, Outlook underlines phone numbers, e-mail addresses, and Web page addresses. The underline tells you that Outlook has checked those entries for obvious errors and found none. (Entering a six-digit phone number would be an obvious error.) In the case of Web page addresses, Outlook not only underlines it but also changes its text to blue to indicate that clicking the entry will start your Web browser and access the Web page. (You may be prompted to connect to the Internet.)

Editing in the workspace

To make one or two minor changes to the information visible in the workspace, simply click an insertion point and make the changes without displaying the Contact window. (In some views, you may not be able to edit certain fields.)

You may have noticed that the Contact window is multi-tabbed. You used the General tab to fill in the information shown earlier. If you want to add more information about a contact, such as an assistant's name or a birthday, you can use the Details tab. (For information about the Activities, Certificates, and All Fields tabs, see the tips below.) Let's add some personal information for Mona Terry, who is not only a colleague, but a friend. Follow these steps:

Recording special occasions

1. Double-click *Terry, Mona* in the workspace and then click the Details tab to display these address-card options:

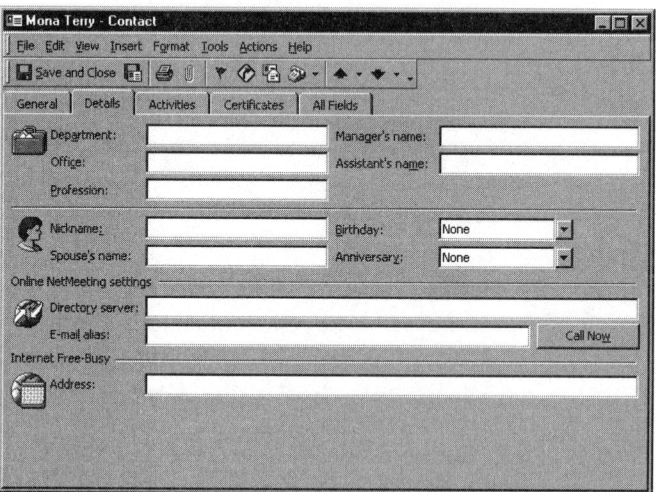

The Activities tab

On the Activities tab, Outlook displays the various options available for tracking your interactions with this contact. Outlook can record activities such as sending e-mail messages and delegating tasks, and upcoming appointments with the contact. The activities are actually tracked in conjunction with Outlook's Journal component, which we discuss in more detail in Chapter 6 (see page 128).

The Certificates tab

Certificates (also called *digital IDs*) are used to maintain secure computing environments. You obtain a certificate from an independent organization such as Verisign, Inc. and then attach it to e-mail messages to prove your identity. To exchange encrypted messages with contacts, they must first send you a message with their certificate attached. Replying to the message stores the certificate in the contact's address card (see Help for more information).

The All Fields tab

On the All Fields tab, Outlook displays the fields available on all the tabs alphabetized in table form. To display the fields organized by category, click the arrow to the right of the Select From box and select the category you want. You can enter information about the contact by typing text in the field's Value column. To create a new field from this tab, click the New button at the bottom of the tab.

2. Click the arrow to the right of the Birthday box to display a small calendar.

3. Use the arrows on either side of the current month's name to navigate to December. Then click 28.

4. Repeat this procedure for the Anniversary box, setting it to August 7.

5. In the Spouse's Name edit box, type *Sandy*. Then click the Save And Close button.

6. Redisplay Mona Terry's address card. The General tab now looks like this:

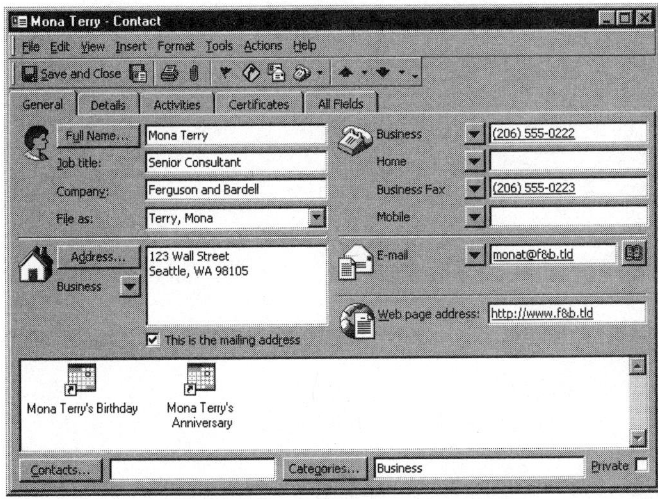

Outlook has created two shortcuts to the Calendar component, indicating that these two dates have been added to your schedule as recurring events. We haven't discussed Calendar yet, so you won't check out these shortcuts now, but you might notice them in certain views of your contact list as attachments to this address card (see page 44).

7. Close the Contact window.

Deleting Contacts

To keep a contact list up-to-date, once in a while you need to delete address cards. Follow the steps on the next page.

1. If your contact list includes a Welcome to Contacts card, click its header to select it, and then click the Delete button.

2. Delete any other contacts you don't want, but be sure to leave the five you just entered. The contact list now looks something like the one shown here:

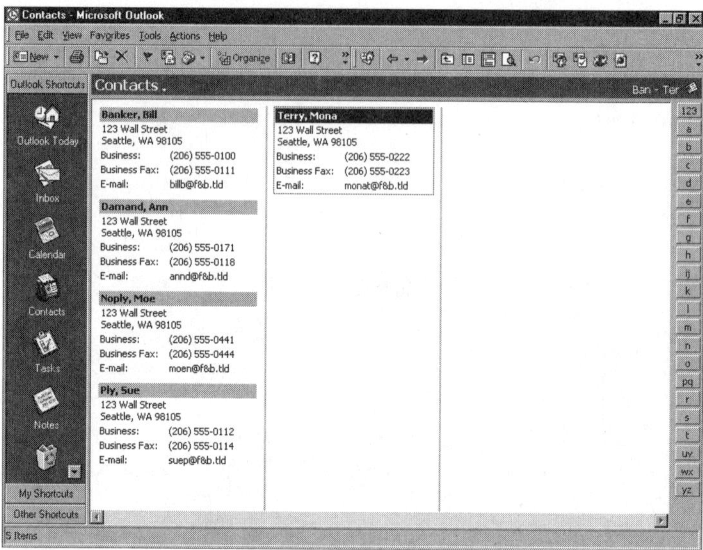

Organizing Contacts

As your contact list grows, you will probably want to organize it so that it is easier to use. In Chapter 1, you looked at different ways to view notes, and many of the techniques you used with Notes can be applied to Contacts. In this section, you will look at other organizational options that are relevant to the Contacts component.

Before you experiment with organizing contacts, add some more address cards to give you a larger contact list to work with. Follow these steps:

1. Click the New Contact button to display the Contact window shown earlier.

2. Enter the names and addresses listed on the facing page, clicking the Save And New button to start a new address card and clicking the Save And Close button after the last entry.

Name	*Ima Tripp*	*Al Pine*	*Rocky Rhode*
Job Title	*President*	*President*	*President*
Company	*Exotic Excursions*	*In the Bag*	*Cream of the Crop*
Bus. Phone	*2065554856*	*9075551454*	*2065551500*
Bus. Fax	*2065554782*	*9075551451*	*2065551501*
Address	*505 West Ave.*	*1200 Yukon Ave.*	*1540 Iceberg Drive*
	Seattle, WA 98115	*Anchorage, AK 99502*	*Seattle, WA 98122*
E-mail	*imat@ee.tld*	*alp@inthebag.tld*	*rockyr@creamcrop.tld*
Web Address	*www.ee.tld*	*www.inthebag.tld*	*www.creamcrop.tld*

Creating New Categories

You've completed all the address cards, and now you need to fine-tune their categories. Some of the contacts you just added are clients, but they are also members of a professional organization you belong to. Let's create a new category for them:

1. Double-click *Tripp, Ima* and then in the Contact window, click the Categories button.
2. In the Item(s) list at the top of the Categories dialog box, type *BusNet* and click Add To List. Outlook adds the new category to the list and puts a check mark in its check box.
3. Click OK to return to the Contact window, and then click Save And Close to save your changes.
4. Now double-click *Pine, Al*, click the Categories button, select BusNet, click OK, and then click Save And Close.
5. Repeat step 4 for Rocky Rhode's card.

Switching Views

By default, Outlook displays the contact list in address cards view, where some of the pertinent information about your contacts appears on index cards that are sorted alphabetically. Because your list is small, you can easily scroll through the cards. However, as a contact list grows, viewing the list in a different way may be more efficient. Let's explore the other views:

1. Click the Advanced toolbar's More Buttons button, click the arrow to the right of the Current View box, and then select Detailed Address Cards from the drop-down list. (When the

The Master Category List

New categories you create in the Categories dialog box are added to the Master Category list. You can add several categories at once by clicking the Master Category List button, typing entries in the New Category box, and clicking Add. You can delete any categories you have created, and you can reset the master category list to include only those categories originally supplied by Outlook.

Advanced toolbar is not displayed, you can choose Current View from the View menu, as you did in Chapter 1.) The address cards now look like this:

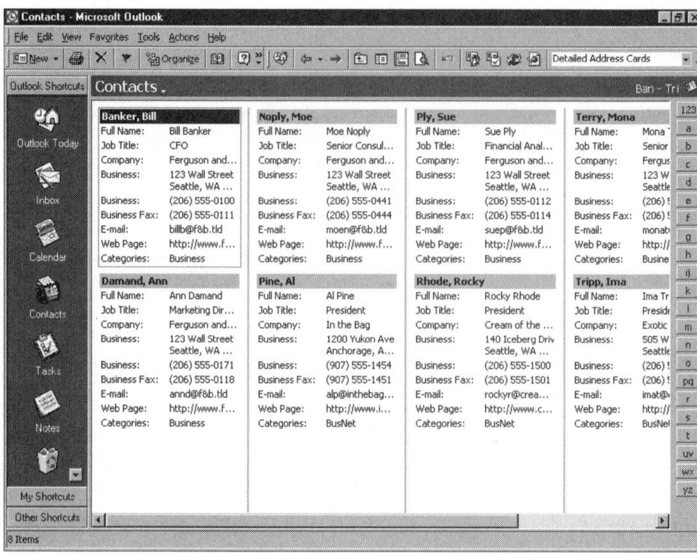

In this view, Outlook displays all the information that was entered on the General tab of the Contact window.

2. Choose Phone List from the Current View drop-down list to display your contacts as shown here:

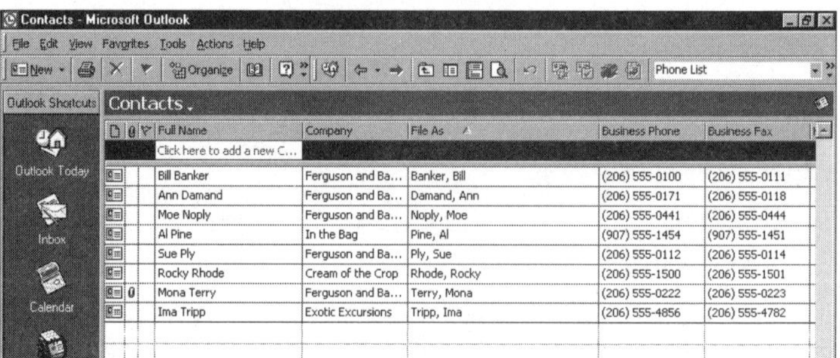

Using the letter tabs

You can jump around in your contact list by clicking the letter tabs along the right side of the Contacts workspace. Clicking a letter does not display only the contacts whose names begin with that letter. Instead, it selects the first contact in your list whose name begins with that or the closest subsequent letter.

This view displays identifying information for each contact as well as four phone columns (which may or may not contain numbers), a Journal column, and a Categories column. (To add a contact in this view, click the Click Here placeholder and type the information.) In a table view, you can see that the contact list is really a database, where the information about a particular contact is stored in a *record* (row) and an individual item of information is stored in a *field* (column).

Records and fields

3. The remaining four table views display contacts sorted by category, company, location, and follow-up tag. Try each view in turn, finishing up with the by category view.

4. If necessary, click the plus sign next to each category to display your contacts like this:

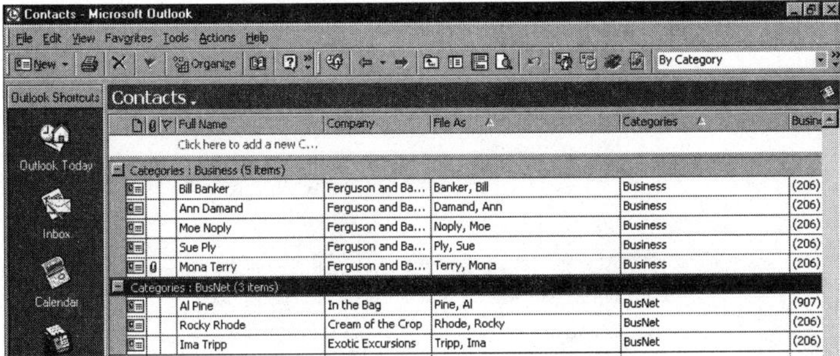

Creating a Custom View

The by category view organizes your contacts conveniently but has a couple of drawbacks: it doesn't display addresses, and it repeats some information. We showed you one method for customizing a view on page 21, but let's try another way:

1. Because you are in by category view, the Categories field is redundant, so get rid of it by right-clicking the Categories column header and choosing Remove This Column from the shortcut menu.

Deleting columns

Flagging contacts for follow-up

If you need to remember something concerning a contact, you can click the contact's flag column in a table view and select Flagged from the drop-down list to display a small flag to the left of the contact's name. You can also select the contact and either click the Flag For Follow Up button on the toolbar or choose Flag For Follow Up from the Actions menu. A dialog box appears in which you can specify why you are flagging the contact and whether the follow-up has to be completed by a specific date. You can remove a flag by right-clicking the flag message or icon and choosing Clear Flag from the shortcut menu.

Sorting in table view

You can sort the information in a table view by clicking the header at the top of the column by which you want Outlook to sort. An arrow appears in the header, pointing up if the column is sorted in ascending order, or down if it is sorted in descending order. Clicking the header again reverses the sort order.

2. Repeat step 1 to remove the empty Home Phone and Mobile Phone columns. (You will need to scroll them into view to delete them.)

Resizing columns

3. To resize the Full Name column so that it is just wide enough to fit the longest name, right-click the column header and then choose Best Fit from the shortcut menu.

4. To resize the File As column, position the mouse pointer over the column header's right border, and then when the pointer changes to a double-headed arrow, double-click the left mouse button. The column instantly adjusts its width to fit the longest entry, and the contact list now looks something like this:

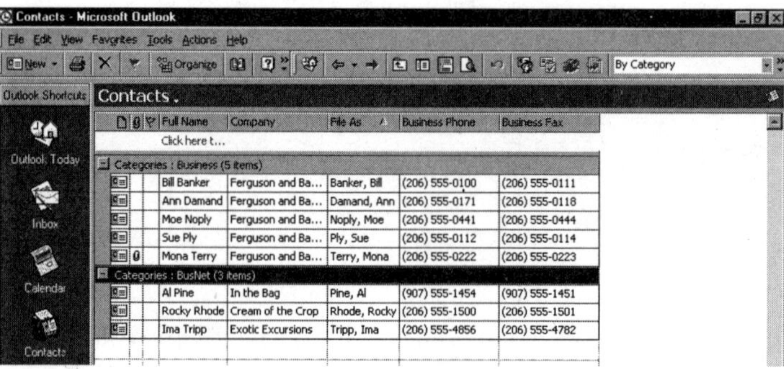

The custom view is starting to take shape, but now you need to add some columns. Follow these steps:

Adding columns

1. To add a column, right-click a column header and then choose Field Chooser from the shortcut menu to display the dialog box shown here:

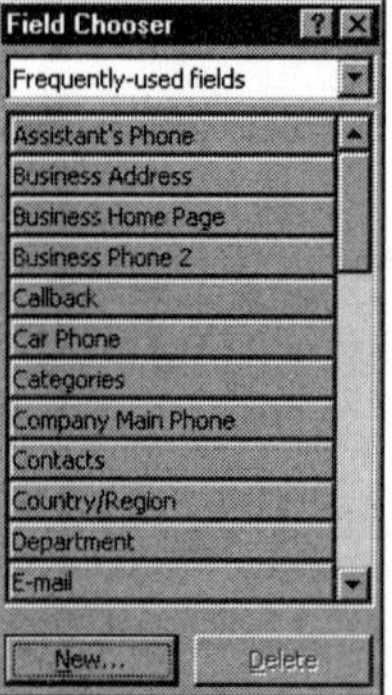

2. Click the Business Address box to select it, point to it, hold down the left mouse button, and drag to the column header row. In the row, a red arrow indicates the new field's location. Release the mouse button when the box sits between the Company and File As column headers.

3. Repeat step 2 to add an E-mail column at the right end of the table. Then click the Field Chooser's Close button.

4. Resize the Business Address and E-mail columns so that they display all of their information.

With those adjustments complete, you're ready to save the current settings as a new view. Follow these steps:

Saving a new view

1. Choose Current View and then Define Views from the View menu to display the dialog box shown earlier on page 23.

2. With Current View Settings selected, click the Copy button to display the Copy View dialog box.

3. Type *New By Category* in the Name Of New View edit box, check All Contact Folders in the Can Be Used On section, and click OK.

4. Click OK in the View Summary dialog box, and click Apply View in the Define Views dialog box.

Restoring a view's settings

5. To restore the original by category view, choose Current View and then Define Views from the View menu. Click By Category in the View list, and click the Reset button. When asked to confirm the restoration, click OK. Then click Close to close the Define Views dialog box.

6. To confirm that the new view is now available, check that New By Category is the selection in the Current View box on the Advanced toolbar.

Creating Your Own Contact Form

On page 40, you added a contact's birthday, anniversary, and spouse's name on the Details tab of the Contact window. As you work with the Contacts component of Outlook, you may find that the General and Details tabs provide some fields that you don't need and yet don't provide some that you do need. To ensure that your contact list includes precisely the fields you want, you can develop a custom contact form.

In this section, you'll develop a custom form for the clients of Ferguson and Bardell. Creating forms in Outlook is similar to creating them in Microsoft Access. If you are familiar with that process, you will recognize the techniques we discuss here. If you are not familiar with the Access process, this section will give you enough experience to experiment later, when you've identified the forms you will need for your work. Let's start by displaying the window where you'll design your form:

Switching to design view

1. Click the New Contact button on the toolbar to display a blank Contact window, and choose Forms and then Design This Form from the window's Tools menu. Outlook displays the Contact window in design view and opens the Field Chooser dialog box, as shown below:

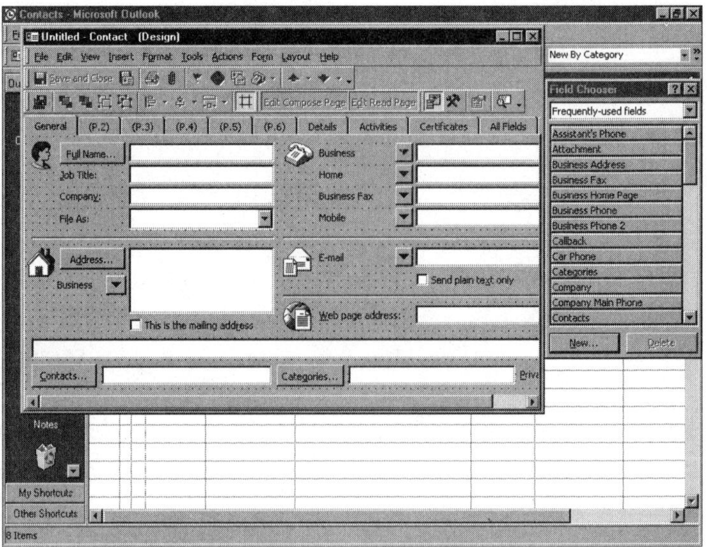

As you can see, the Contact window has more tabs in design view than in data entry view.

2. Click the (P.2) tab to display a blank second page.

You can design the form by dragging fields from the Field Chooser dialog box to the page displayed in the window. But if none of the predefined fields fits the bill, you can create new fields. Let's add some new fields now:

Creating new fields

1. In the Field Chooser dialog box, click the New button to display this New Field dialog box:

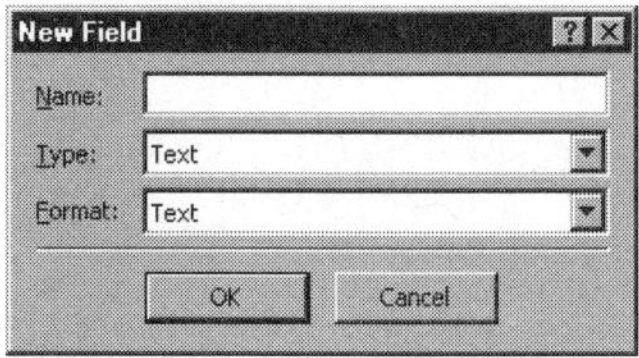

2. Type *Date Acquired* in the Name edit box.

3. Click the arrow to the right of the Type box and select Date/Time from the drop-down list.

4. Select the short date format (7/1/99, for example) from the Format drop-down list and click OK. In the Field Chooser dialog box, Outlook displays the User-Defined Fields In Folder group and adds a Date Acquired field box to the group list.

5. Repeat steps 1 through 4 to add the fields shown here:

Name	*Amount Invested*	*Annual Report Due Date*	*Wiring Instructions*
Type	*Currency*	*Date/Time*	*Text*
Format	*Dollars and cents*	*Short date*	*Text*

To add the new fields to the blank form, follow these steps:

Adding fields to a new form

1. Click the Date Acquired field in the Field Chooser dialog box and drag it anywhere on the blank form. When you release the mouse button, Outlook positions the new field in the top left corner of the form.

2. Next drag the Amount Invested field onto the form. Outlook positions the field below the Date Acquired field.

3. Drag the Annual Report Due Date and Wiring Instructions fields onto the form and then close the Field Chooser dialog box. The form now looks like the one on the next page.

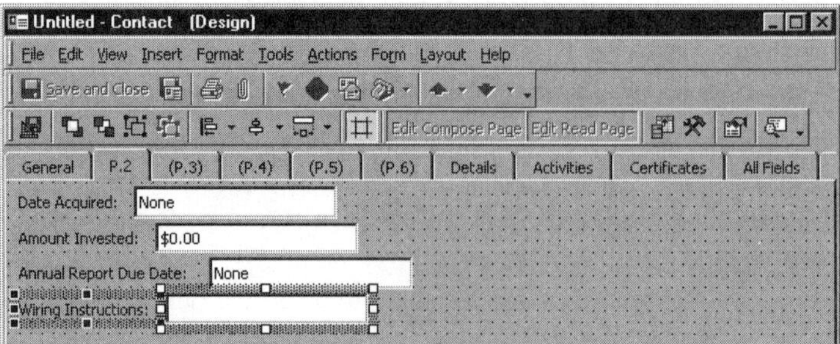

Labels and controls

The form is made up of two types of boxes. The boxes containing the field names are called *labels*, and the white boxes—where you will enter data in the new form—are called *controls*.

Moving Controls and Labels

Moving the fields onto the new form was easy enough, but Outlook has simply dumped everything in the top left corner. Let's line up the controls to make them easier to work with:

Handles

1. Click the white control to the right of Date Acquired. Small squares called *handles* appear around the control's border, indicating that it is selected.

2. Hold down the Ctrl key and click the three remaining control boxes so that all of them are selected, like this:

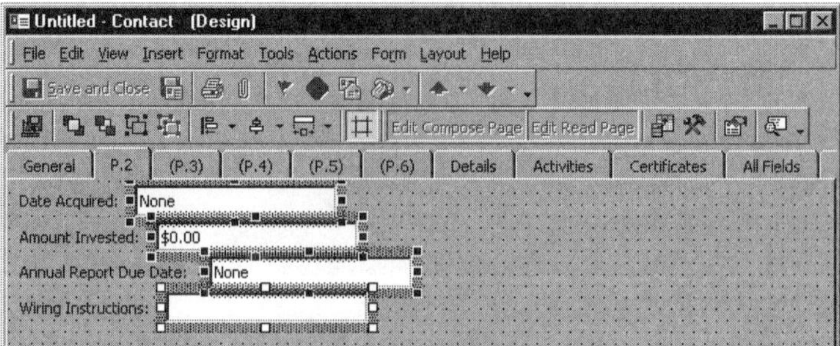

The Align Left button

3. Choose Align and then Left from the Layout menu. (You can also click the Align Left button on the Design toolbar; you might have to click the arrow to the right of the Align button and select Left.) Outlook aligns all the selected controls to the left, as shown on the facing page.

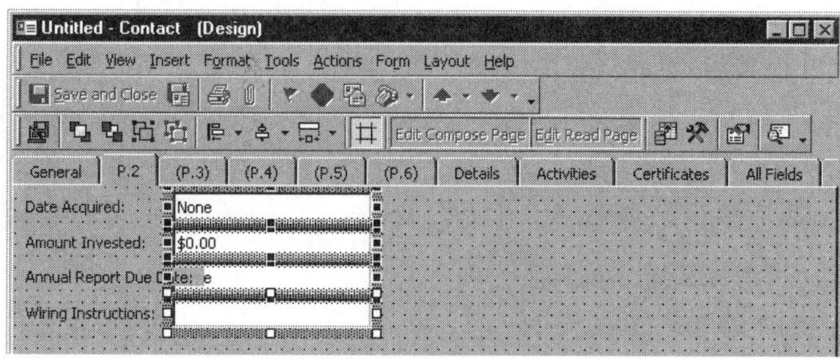

The Annual Report Due Date label partially obscures its control. To fix this problem, you can fine-tune the position of the controls with the mouse, like this:

Moving controls

1. With the controls still selected, point to any border (not a handle). When the pointer changes to a four-headed arrow, hold down the left mouse button and drag the controls to the right by at least three gridline markers.

The Snap To Grid button

2. If you have trouble keeping the controls aligned with their labels, click the Snap To Grid button to toggle it off. Then adjust the position of the controls as necessary. The result is shown here:

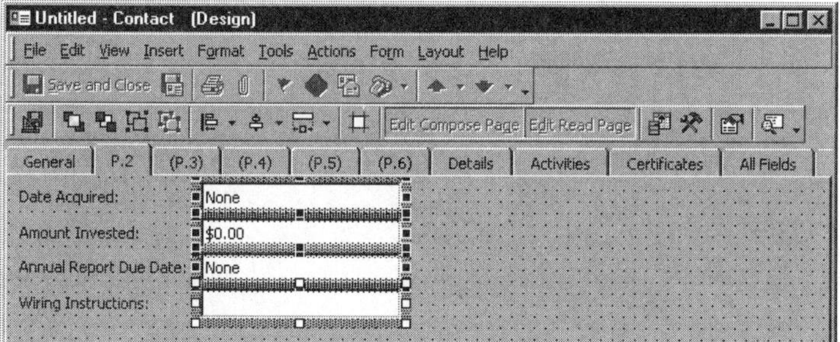

Sizing Controls and Labels

The sizes of the first three controls on the new form are fine, but you need to make the last control larger in order to display lengthy instructions for wiring money. You should also resize the first, second, and fourth labels so that they are the same width as the Annual Report Due Date label. Follow the steps on the next page to resize these items now.

More layout options

When creating a custom contact form, you may want to explore some of the other available commands on the Layout menu. For example, you can adjust the space between objects by selecting the objects and then using the Horizontal Spacing or Vertical Spacing commands. You can quickly size objects to the width of their text by selecting the object and choosing Size To Fit from the Layout menu. If you don't like the effect of a particular command, choose Undo from the Edit menu.

1. Click away from the controls to deselect them, and then select the Wiring Instructions control.

2. Point to the bottom middle handle. When the pointer changes to a double-headed arrow, hold down the left mouse button and then drag downward until the box approximately triples in size.

3. To make all the labels the same size as the Annual Report Due Date label, select the other three labels by clicking each in turn while holding down the Ctrl key. While still holding the Ctrl key, select the Annual Report Due Date label. (You must select this label last.) Release the Ctrl key.

The Make Same Width button

4. Click the Make Same Width button on the Design toolbar to tell Outlook to resize all the labels to match the last label you selected. Click away from the labels to deselect them and view the form, which now looks like this:

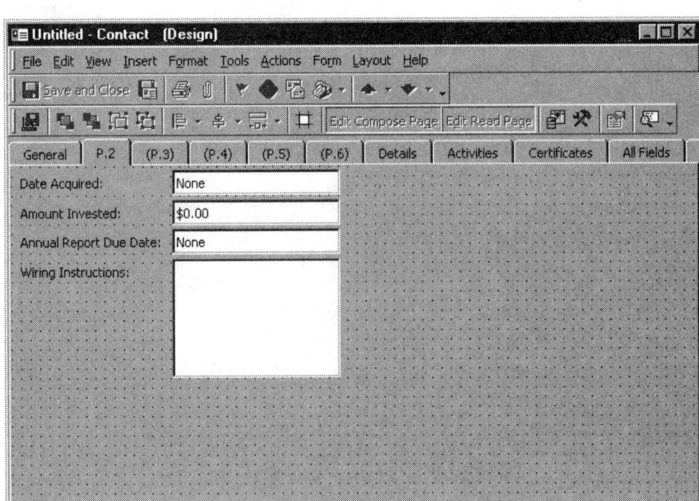

Saving a New Form

This simple form is now complete, and all you have to do is save it so that you can begin to use it. But first you'll give the form's tab a more descriptive name than P.2. Follow the steps on the facing page.

The Toolbox

When creating custom forms, you might want to use the Toolbox, which is displayed when you click the Control Toolbox button on the Design toolbar. You can use the Toolbox buttons to add different types of controls to a form. For example, you can add text boxes, labels, option buttons, check boxes, graphics, and frames. You might want to explore these tools and practice adding form objects. Check the Help feature for details about these tools so that you can use them to create forms that meet your needs.

1. Choose Rename Page from the expanded Form menu to display this dialog box:

Renaming a page

2. Type *Account Details* as the name and then click OK. Outlook displays the new name on the tab.

3. To save the new form, click the Publish Form button at the left end of the Design toolbar. Because Outlook won't let you change its default contact form, it displays this dialog box so that you can save the form with a different name:

The Publish Form button

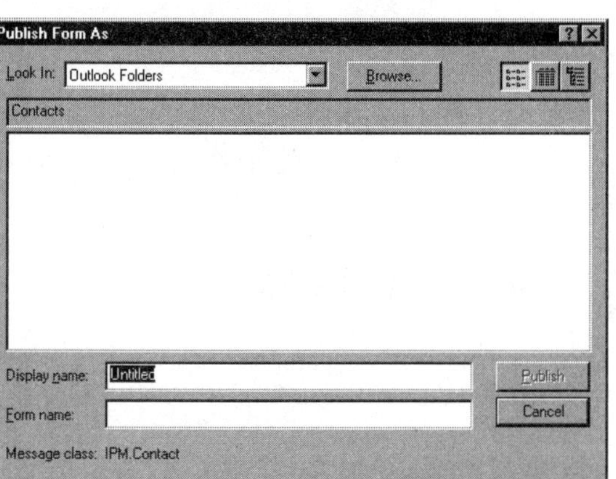

4. Type *Client Form* in the Display Name edit box. Outlook assumes this is also the form's name and enters it in the Form Name edit box, but you can easily enter a different name there if you want.

5. With Outlook Folders in the Look In box and Contacts in the header above the empty list box, click Publish.

Filling In Custom Forms

Now that you have created and saved the custom form, you can use it to enter a new contact. Follow the steps at the top of the next page.

Hiding form pages

If you want to keep a custom form simple by not displaying some tabs in the Contact window, click a tab to display it in design view and then choose Display This Page from the Form menu to toggle the command off. Tabs with names in parentheses—(P.3), for example—are not displayed in the Contact window unless you have customized them, so you can hide only the General, Details, Journal, Certificates, and All Fields tabs.

1. Choose Run This Form from the Form menu. Outlook opens a Contact window that reflects the work you just finished.
2. On the General tab, enter the following contact information:

Name	*Mary Gold*
Job Title	*President*
Company	*Terra Firm*
Bus. Phone	*3195558563*
Bus. Fax	*3195558560*
Address	*1440 West Dogwood Road* *Cedar Rapids, IA 52401*
E-mail	*maryg@t-firm.tld*
Web Address	*www.t-firm.tld*
Category	*BusNet*

3. Click the Account Details tab, and in the Date Acquired box, replace the word *None* with *5/5/93*.
4. Press Tab and type *14200000*. Then press Tab again, type *10/15/99*, press Tab, and type *Send to Woodgrove Bank*. The Account Details tab now looks like this:

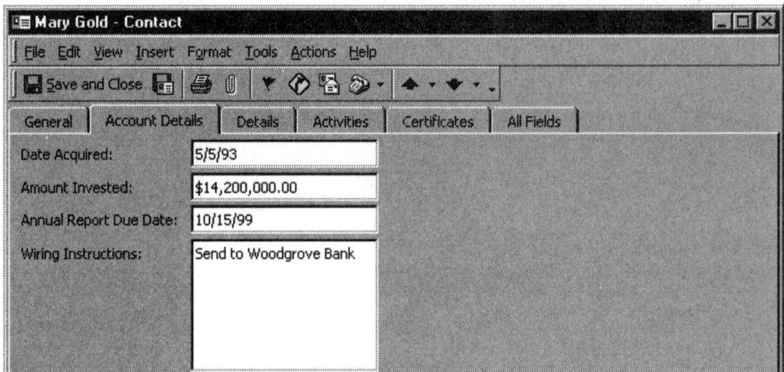

5. Now click Save And Close to close the new contact.
6. Click the window's Close button, clicking No to discard the blank address card you opened on page 48.

To use the custom client form to enter new contacts, choose New Client Form from the expanded Actions menu instead of clicking the New Contact button. To set your custom form as the default used by the New Contact button, right-click the

Editing custom forms

To edit an existing custom form, open it by choosing it from the Actions menu. Switch to design view by choosing Forms and then Design This Form from the Tools menu. Make any editing adjustments and click the Publish Form button on the Design toolbar to save the form with the changes.

Contacts icon in the Outlook bar and choose Properties. On the General tab, select Client Form from the When Posting drop-down list, and click OK.

Using Contacts to Write a Letter

As you work through the rest of this book, we will introduce ways to use the contact list to speed up other Outlook tasks, such as sending an e-mail message, planning a meeting, or adding a new task. Also, after you develop a contact list, whenever you write letters or create mailing labels in Microsoft Word, you can use the Address Book to enter information instead of typing it from scratch. (See the tip on the next page.)

If you are working in Outlook, you don't have to manually open Word to write a letter. You can go directly from Outlook to a Word document and have the Letter Wizard walk you through the steps of creating the letter. When you have finished, the wizard generates the skeleton of the letter in the Word document, and you can then enter the text. Follow these steps to compose a letter to Al Pine:

The Letter Wizard

1. With Contacts open in the workspace, click the Al Pine record once to select it.
2. Choose New Letter To Contact from the Actions menu. Word starts the Letter Wizard, which displays its first dialog box:

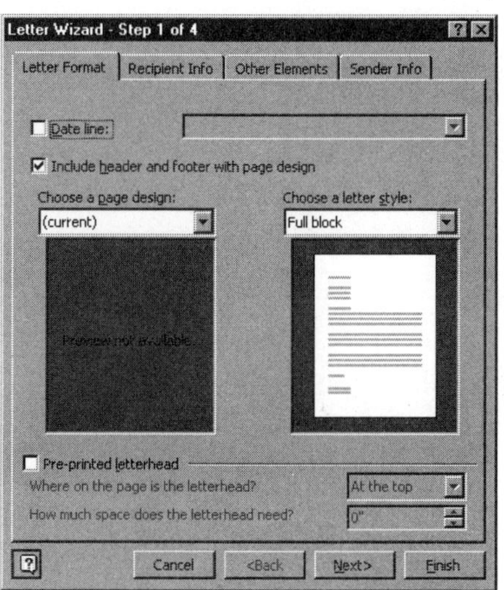

Deleting custom forms

To delete a custom contact form, right-click the Contacts icon in the Outlook bar, choose Properties, click the Forms tab, and then click the Manage button. In the Form Manager dialog box, select the form you want to remove and click the Delete button. Click Yes to confirm the deletion and close the dialog boxes.

3. Click the Date Line check box so that the letter displays the current date in the format shown in the box to its right. (You can select a different format from the box's drop-down list.)

4. Click the arrow to the right of the Choose A Page Design box and check out the page design options. (Included are Word templates such as Contemporary Letter and Elegant Letter.) Then select Professional Letter from the list.

5. In the Choose A Letter Style box, check that Full Block is selected. (The Letter Wizard displays a preview of the style in the box below the Style box.)

6. Click the Pre-Printed Letterhead check box at the bottom of the dialog box and use the up arrow in the right corner to tell the wizard to allow 1" at the top of the page for a preprinted letterhead. Then click Next to display the Recipient Info tab of the Letter Wizard, as shown below:

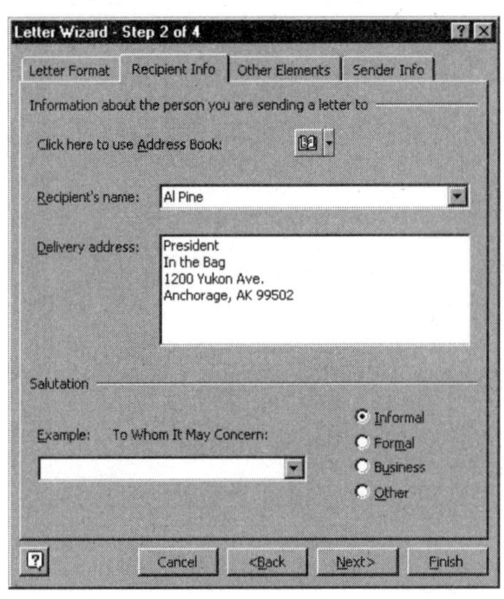

7. Read over the recipient information, check that the Informal option is selected in the Salutation section, and type *Dear Al:* in the edit box. Then click Next to display the Other Elements tab shown on the facing page.

Using the Address Book in Word

Outlook's Address Book stores the information entered in the Contact window. (Other available address books usually include the Global Address List created and maintained by your company.) Provided the Outlook Address Book is included in the list of services in the active profile, your contact list is one of the address books available when you create mailing labels in Word. (Choose Services from the Tools menu to check your services list, and then click the Add button if you need to add Outlook Address Book to your profile.) To create labels or form letters using your contact list, use Word's mail-merge feature. When you click the Get Data button in the Mail Merge Helper dialog box, choose the Use Address Book option and select the Outlook Address Book. Then continue following the normal mail-merge procedure. (If you need help with mail-merge, consult Word's Help feature.) If you want to easily insert one of your contact's addresses in a Word document, you can do so by adding an Insert Address button to a Word toolbar. (For information on adding buttons to toolbars, see the Help feature.)

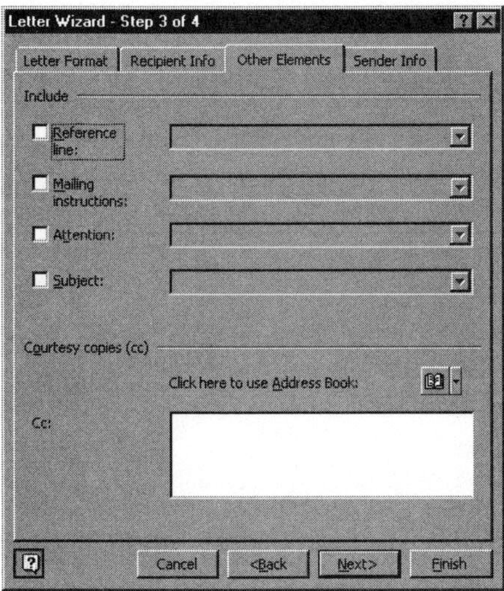

8. Click the Reference Line check box, click the arrow to the right of its box, and select RE:.

9. Click an insertion point to the right of RE: in the edit box, press the Spacebar, and then type *Monthly Lecture Series*. Click Next to display the fourth tab, shown here:

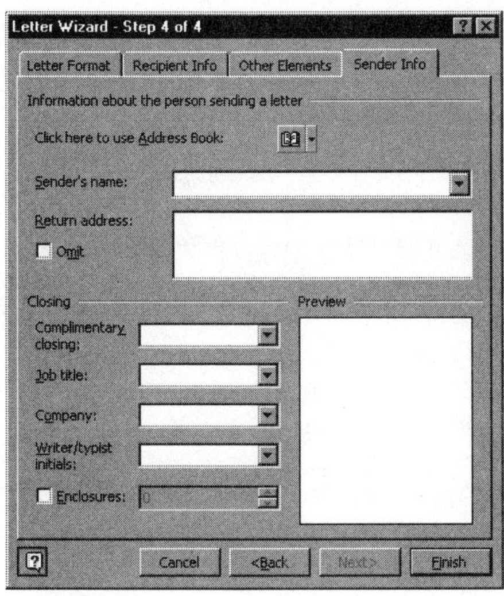

Calling a contact

If a modem is hooked up to your computer, you can have Outlook dial the phone numbers of your contacts for you. With Contacts displayed in the workspace, select the contact you want to call and choose Call Contact from the expanded Actions menu to display a submenu of commands. Included on the list are the phone numbers for this contact, a New Call command that you can use to dial a different number, and Redial and Speed Dial commands. Choosing a phone number displays the New Call dialog box. To have Journal track the phone call, click the Create New Journal Entry check box. (See the tip on page 131 for more information.) To dial the number, click the Start Call button. When the Call Status dialog box appears, pick up the receiver and then click the Talk button. When you finish the call, hang up the receiver, click the End Call button, and then click Close in the New Call dialog box.

10. Type your name in the Sender's Name box. Then click the arrow to the right of the Complimentary Closing box and select Sincerely from the drop-down list. Click Finish to display the letter in Word, as shown below. (If necessary, click Cancel to close the Office Assistant.)

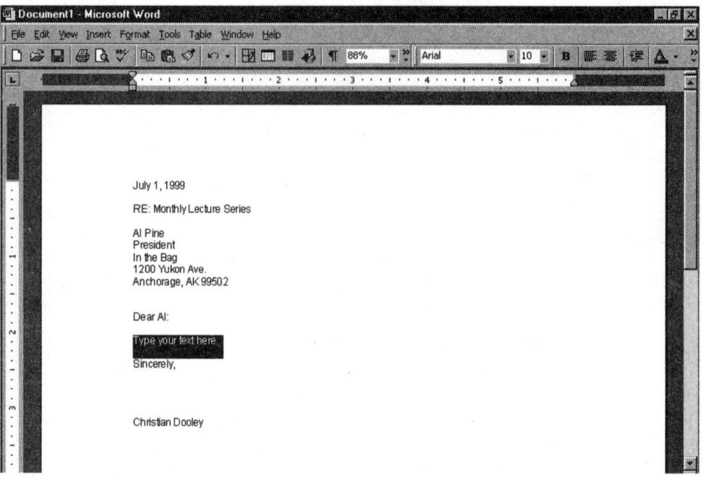

11. You won't actually type the text of the letter now, so click Word's Close button to close the program and the letter, and click No when asked about saving changes.

Displaying Address Map

If your computer can access the Internet, you can pinpoint the exact location of an address by using the Address Map feature. Open the Contact window for a contact, and click the Display Map Of Address button on the Contact window's toolbar. Internet Explorer (or your Web browser) starts, connects to the Internet, and takes you to the Microsoft Expedia Web site, which displays a map of the address in the Contact window open on your screen. You can then print the map.

Printing the contact list

Using Outlook eliminates some of the need for paper printouts, but when you do want a printout of your contact list, click the Print button to display the Print dialog box. You can select from several layout choices in the Print Style section, and you can click the Page Setup button to make adjustments on the Format, Paper, or Header/Footer tabs. On the Paper tab of the Page Setup dialog box, you can change the Type setting in the Paper section to Avery Labels or FiloFax. In the Page section, you can change the Size setting to fit special formats for Franklin Planners, Day Timers, or Day Runners. You can also click the Define Styles button to make permanent edits to a particular style or to copy a style. As you make modifications, you can check what the printout will look like by clicking the Print Preview button. In print preview, the mouse pointer changes to a magnifying glass. Click the mouse button once to zoom in on the page and click again to zoom back out. When you are ready to print, simply click OK in the Print dialog box.

The Letter Wizard gives you some idea of the ways you can streamline your work by using the contact list. As we said, you will be looking at other methods throughout this book.

With this chapter under your belt, you're well on your way to managing all your contacts with the efficiency only a computer can offer. And remember, if you want to use Outlook to its full potential, be sure to keep your contact list up-to-date!

3 Communicating with E-Mail

Whether you're working on a stand-alone computer or on a network, this chapter shows you how to use Outlook's e-mail component to send, read, and respond to e-mail messages. Then you learn ways to organize messages for maximum efficiency.

E-mail is no longer just a means of business communication, and the techniques you learn in this chapter can be applied to all forms of correspondence, whether you are writing to a colleague, a teacher, or a friend.

Tasks performed and concepts covered:

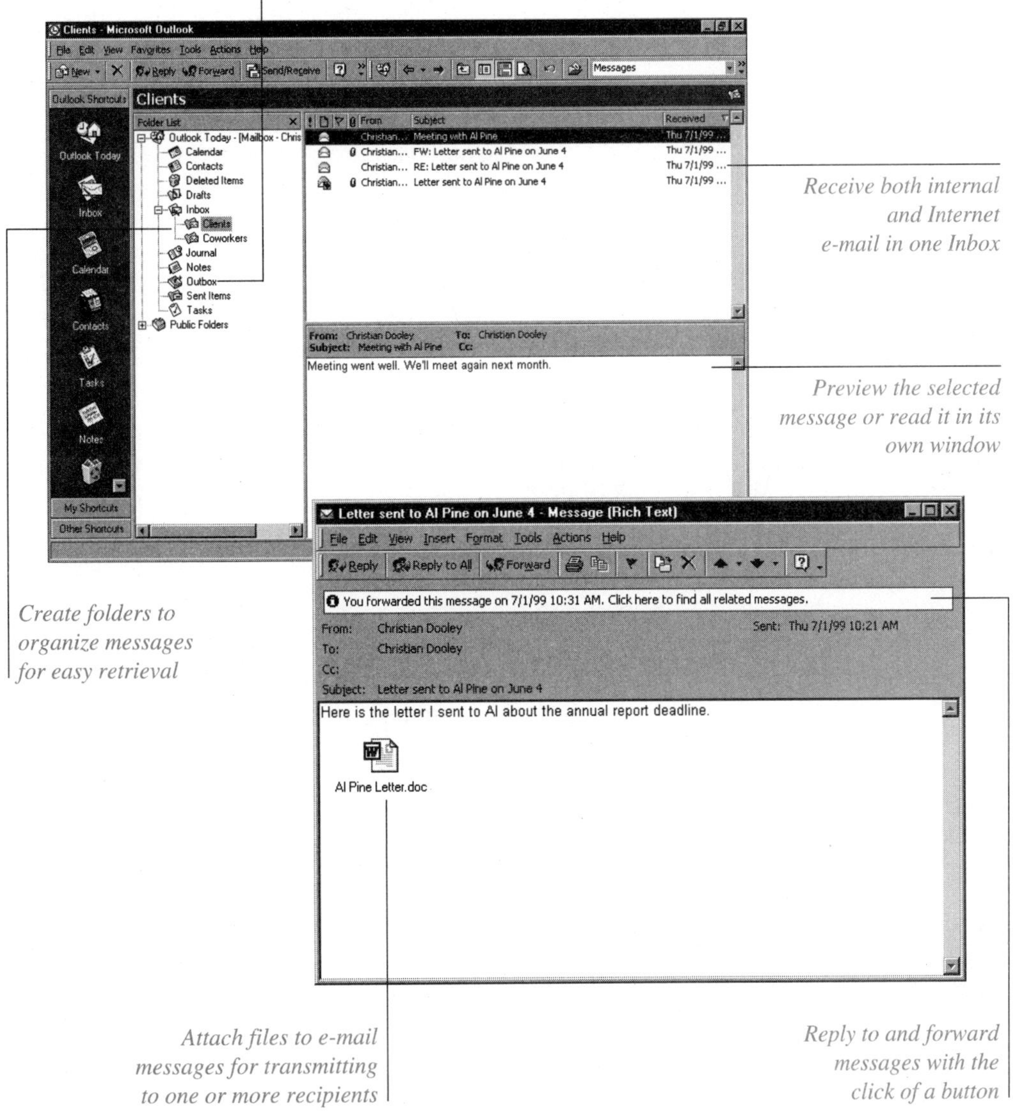

Outlook's Contacts component, discussed in Chapter 2, helps you organize information about people without actually communicating with them. But communication with colleagues is an integral part of daily work, and in recent years, electronic mail (or *e-mail*) has become the primary method of communication for many people. Some people have internal e-mail (company-wide or institution-wide), some have Internet e-mail, and some have both. Regardless of what type of e-mail you have, it can all be handled by Outlook's e-mail component. In this chapter, we discuss how to use this component to create, send, receive, and manage e-mail messages.

There's nothing difficult about the concept of e-mail. It's simply a way of sending messages that bypasses the traditional post office. The beauty of e-mail is that it doesn't use paper resources, it's fast, and it costs nothing (at least, nothing more than you may already be paying for Internet access). Sometimes it is even better than using the telephone because you can deal with important business right away rather than running the risk of playing phone tag. Add to these advantages the fact that you can include files, programs, and other attachments with the messages you send, and also that you can send the same message to several people without any additional effort. It's not surprising that even people with abysmal letter-writing habits become staunch advocates of e-mail as a means of communication.

Sometimes people confuse internal e-mail and Internet e-mail. It's easy to understand why because, in many ways, they are

Setting up Internet e-mail

If you work for a large organization or you access the Internet through a school computer, e-mail has probably already been set up on your computer. But if you are working on a stand-alone computer, you can't send or receive Internet e-mail in Outlook until you set it up. First you will need to obtain the domain names of your outgoing and incoming e-mail servers from your ISP. Then start the Internet Connection Wizard by choosing Settings and then Control Panel from the Start menu, double-clicking the Internet Options icon, and then clicking the Connections tab of the Internet Properties dialog box. Click the Connect button to start the wizard. As you work through the dialog boxes, you will need to enter information such as your e-mail address, account name, and password. If you need help with this setup, contact your ISP. If you already have a Dial-Up Networking connection to your ISP, you may need to add the Internet E-Mail service to your Outlook profile. Choose Services from the Tools menu and then complete all the tabs of the dialog box to set up this service.

similar. However, having internal e-mail doesn't necessarily mean you have Internet e-mail, and vice versa. To be able to send e-mail to a colleague down the hall via internal e-mail, both your computer and your colleague's computer need to be connected to your organization's network. To be able to send e-mail to a client in another state via the Internet, both your computer and your client's computer need to be able to access the Internet. This access may be invisibly provided by a server on your network, further blurring the distinction between internal and Internet e-mail. Or access may be more visibly provided via a modem connection to an *Internet service provider* (or *ISP*). Either way, you can use Outlook. (See the tip on the facing page for more information about Internet e-mail.) Outlook can be configured to work with many of the more popular e-mail programs, but to take full advantage of some of Outlook's capabilities, you need to be working on a network that runs Microsoft Exchange Server.

Using the Inbox

As you may recall from Chapter 1, by default the Inbox is the component displayed in the workspace when you start Outlook. The Inbox is Outlook's main e-mail folder and the place where you will spend most of your time when working with e-mail. (Icons for the other e-mail folders—Drafts, Outbox, and Sent Items—are available in the Outlook bar's My Shortcuts group.) Well, let's jump right in and start sending and receiving messages:

1. Start Outlook by double-clicking its icon on the desktop. One of two things happens:

- If Outlook is set up to automatically log on to an e-mail server when it starts up, Outlook connects to the server and then checks for new messages.
- If Outlook is not set up to automatically log on to an e-mail server, Outlook does not connect to your server. (By the way, this method is called *working offline*.) Don't worry though. You can still proceed, and we will show you how to manually make the connection on page 69.

The Drafts folder

When you are composing an important e-mail message (or one that's very long), you may need to pause to do a little research or maybe just to take a break. You can choose the File menu's Save command to store the unfinished message in the Drafts folder. Then when you're ready to resume, double-click the message in the Drafts folder to reopen the Message window with all the information you've already entered intact. You can then finish the message and send it on its way.

The Inbox icon

If you have been working in another Outlook component, you can display the contents of the Inbox in the workspace by clicking the Inbox icon in the Outlook bar's Outlook Shortcuts group.

Composing Messages

With Outlook, you both send and receive e-mail through the Inbox. You'll practice the sending side of the equation first. For demonstration purposes, you will e-mail a reminder message to yourself, but bear in mind that you would probably use Outlook's Notes or Tasks component for this type of reminder, rather than e-mail. In our examples, we use internal e-mail, but if you are using Internet e-mail, you should have no difficulty following along.

Suppose you are planning a meeting with a client and you want to remind yourself to check on the conference room reservation first thing tomorrow morning. Follow these steps:

The New Mail Message button

Message formats

You can send messages in one of three formats. The simplest is Plain Text, which you use when you don't know which e-mail program your message recipients have. Outlook Rich Text format can handle some text formatting, and can be used to send messages to other Outlook users. HTML format can handle more complex formatting but can't be interpreted by some e-mail programs. To specify a default format, choose Options from the Tools menu, click the Mail Format tab, and make a selection from the Send In This Message Format drop-down list. To change the format of a specific message, choose the relevant command from the Format menu.

1. Click the New Mail Message button on the toolbar to display a Message window like the one shown here:

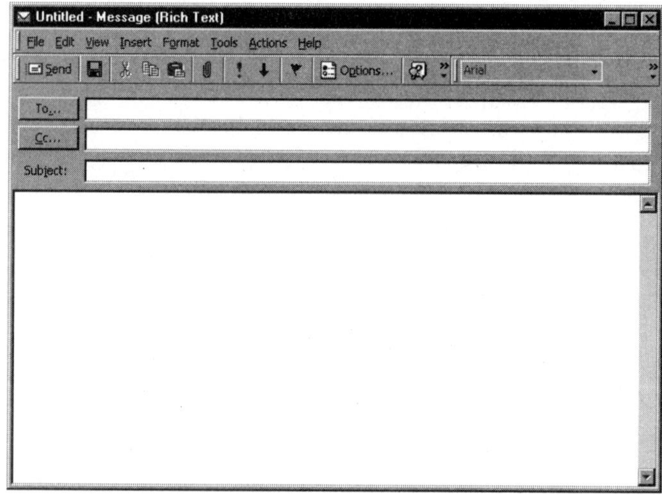

2. In the To edit box, type your own e-mail address. (To send a message to someone else instead, enter his or her address. To send the same message to more than one person, enter their addresses one after the other, separated by semicolons.) Then press Tab to move to the next box.

3. To send a courtesy copy of the message, you can enter the name of the recipient in the Cc edit box. For this message, leave the Cc edit box blank by pressing Tab.

Sending courtesy copies

4. Next type *Confirm conference room reservation* in the Subject edit box and press Tab.

Specifying the subject

5. Enter the message itself in the blank area at the bottom of the window. Type the following: *Check on conference room B reservation. It should be reserved at 1:00 PM for two hours. Make sure overhead projector is set up*. The window now looks like this:

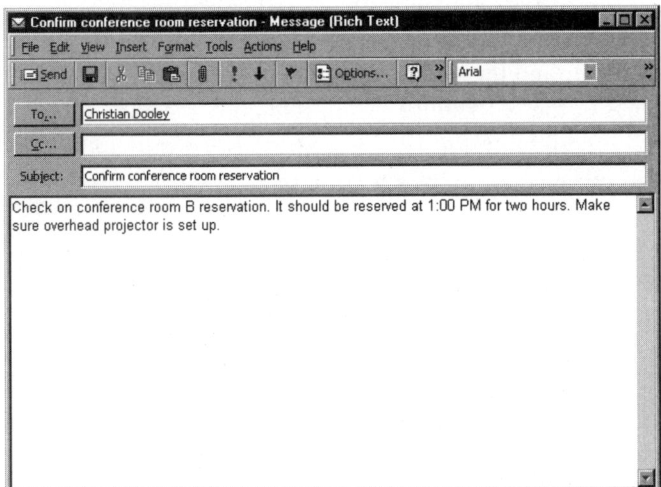

Message options

When composing a new message, you can set options by clicking the Options button on the Message window's toolbar. In the Message Settings section, specify the importance and sensitivity levels of the message. Specifying the importance level as high displays an exclamation mark in the message's header. (You can also set the importance level by clicking the Importance: High or Importance: Low buttons on the toolbar.) You can set the sensitivity level to Normal, Personal, Private, or Confidential. In the Security section, select Encrypt Contents And Attachments to make a message's contents readable only by its recipients and select Add Digital Signature to verify that you are the sender of the message. (You need a digital ID to implement security; see the Help feature.) In the Voting And Tracking Options section, set voting options (see the tip on the next page) and specify notification options. In the Delivery Options section, specify locations for replies and for the sent message, and set a delivery date/time and an expiration date for the message. (The message is deleted if not opened by this date.) Also on this tab, you can assign a message to a category by clicking the Categories button and making a selection.

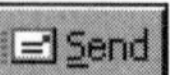

The Send button

6. Send the message by clicking the Send button. Outlook closes the Message window and does one of two things:

- If you are connected to your e-mail server, Outlook transfers the message to the Outbox and then sends it to the server. The server then sends the message to the recipient. In this case, it will send the message back to you because your own e-mail address is in the To edit box.
- If you are not connected to your e-mail server, Outlook stores the message in the Outbox, where it waits until your next connection is made.

The Outbox icon

7. If you are in the latter group, confirm that the message is waiting to be sent by clicking the My Shortcuts button on the Outlook bar and then clicking the Outbox icon to display its contents in the workspace. Then redisplay the Inbox's contents by displaying the Outlook Shortcuts group and clicking the Inbox icon on the Outlook bar.

Adding a signature

To have information, such as your name, job title, company name, or slogan, automatically added to the end of all of your messages, you can create a signature. (Avoid cutesy pictures or sayings as they become tiresome rather quickly.) Choose Options from the Tools menu. On the Mail Format tab, click the Signature Picker button, and click New. Enter a name for the signature and click Next. Type your information in the text box, format it, and click Finish. Click OK in the Signature Picker dialog box, verify the default signature, and click OK. You can set up different signatures for different types of messages. To change the default signature for a specific message, click the Signature button and make your selection.

Using virtual business cards (vcards)

You can pass on the information in a contact's address card via e-mail with a virtual business card, or vcard. First display the contents of Contacts, and then select the contact whose information you want to pass on. Choose Forward As Vcard from the Actions menu, and Outlook displays a Message window with an icon for the contact. Enter the recipient and subject information as usual, type your message, and then send it on its way. Anyone who opens the message can double-click the icon to display the address card for the contact, add any additional information, and click Save And Close to save the information in their own contact list.

Voting

You can send e-mail messages with voting buttons to get input from your colleagues about anything from officer elections to the venue for the company picnic. Display a new Message window and then click the Options button on the toolbar. Click the Use Voting Buttons check box in the Voting And Tracking Options section, and click the arrow to the right of its edit box to select voting button names. To use your own names, type them in the edit box, separating them with semicolons. Click Close and then send the message. When the message is opened, Outlook shows the voting buttons at the top of the window. Recipients click the desired button and send the response with or without editing it.

Addressing Messages Quickly

Most people spend a lot of their e-mailing time sending messages to the same group of people. We discussed the Contacts component in Chapter 2 so that when you got to this chapter, you would already have a contact list to serve as a database of people you deal with repeatedly. When you have a contact list available, tasks such as sending e-mail messages become much easier. Let's send another message, this time using the contact list to speed up the process. Try this:

1. First add an address card for yourself to the contact list, entering just your name and e-mail address. (If you need a refresher on creating address cards, see page 37.)

2. Next display the Inbox and click the New Mail Message button to display a window like the one shown on page 64.

3. Click the To button in the window to display the Select Names dialog box.

Selecting a name from a list

4. When you are working on a network, by default Outlook displays the Global Address List—all the e-mail addresses maintained by your e-mail server. To see a list of your contacts, click the arrow to the right of the Show Names From The box and then select Contacts under Outlook Address Book. The dialog box changes to look something like this:

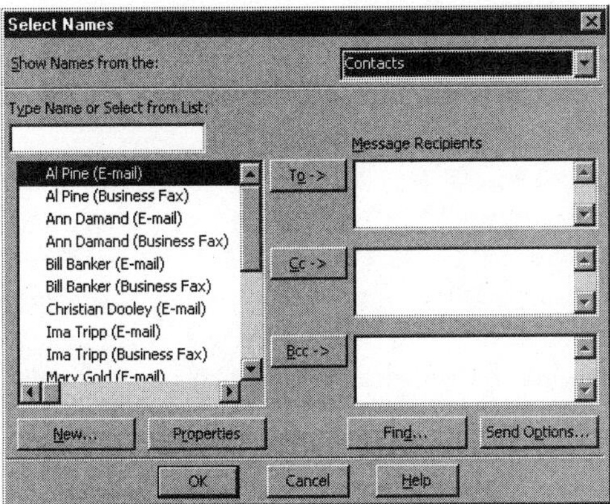

5. Select your e-mail entry from the list. Click the To button to add your e-mail address to the Message Recipients box. Then

Internal vs. Internet setup

A quick reminder: we wrote this book using a networked computer with internal e-mail. If you are working on a stand-alone computer configured for Internet e-mail, some of the dialog boxes you'll see may be a bit different from those we show. Also, you'll see Internet e-mail names, which include an @ sign followed by a domain name as well as a user name (for example, monat@f&b.tld).

click OK to close the dialog box and redisplay the Message window with your name entered in the To box.

6. Fill in the Subject box, type a message to yourself, and then click the Send button. (If you are not logged on to your e-mail server, the Outbox now contains two messages to be sent.)

Attaching Files to Messages

With Outlook, you can send files with your messages. Suppose you want to send a letter created in Word to a colleague. The following steps, which use your own e-mail address instead of a colleague's, demonstrate the process:

1. With the Inbox active, click the New Mail Message button and then either type your e-mail address in the To edit box or use the To button to insert the address.
2. In the Subject box, type *Letter sent to Al Pine on June 4* and press Tab.
3. Next, in the message area, type *Here is the letter I sent to Al about the annual report deadline.*

The Insert File button

4. Press Enter twice to add some space, and then click the Insert File button on the toolbar to display a dialog box similar to the one shown on the facing page.

E-mailing contacts

To send an e-mail message to one of your contacts, simply right-click the appropriate address card in Contacts and then choose New Message To Contact from the shortcut menu. Outlook displays a Message window with the contact's e-mail address already entered in the To edit box. Complete the other edit boxes in the Message window, type the message, and then click the Send button to send the message.

Using distribution lists

If you frequently send messages to a specific group of people, you can set up a distribution list so that typing the list's name in the To box of the Message window sends the message to everyone on the list. To set up a list, click the Address Book button on the toolbar and then click the New Entry button on the Address Book window's toolbar. In the New Entry dialog box, select New Distribution List and click OK. Then in the Distribution List window, type a name for the list, click Select Members, select each person, click Add, and then click OK. Click the Save And Close button to close the Distribution List window and then close the Address Book window. To create a message addressed to the people on the list, open a new Message window, click the To button, double-click the distribution list name, and click OK. When you click the Send button, Outlook sends a copy of the message to everyone on the list.

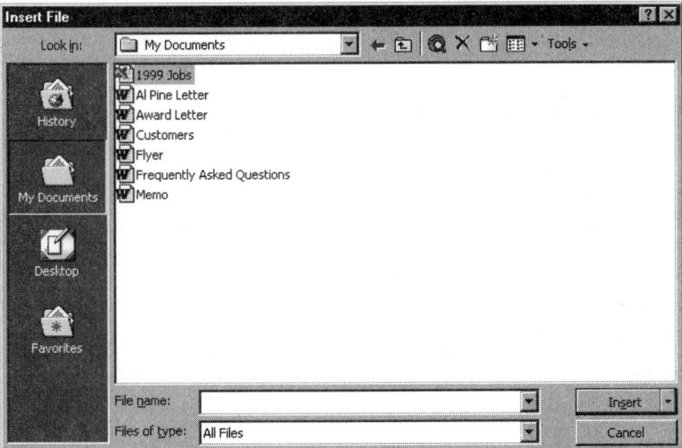

5. Select a short document and click Insert. (You can click the arrow to the right of the Insert button to insert the document as text in the message, or to attach a shortcut to the document, rather than attaching the document itself.) Outlook inserts a file icon, similar to the one shown here:

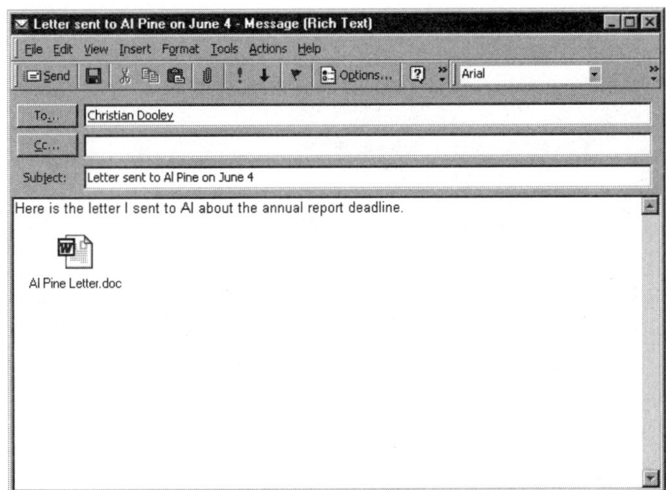

6. Click the Send button.

Sending and Retrieving Messages

If you are connected to your e-mail server, you now have three new message headers displayed in the workspace. If you aren't connected, you need to log on and send the messages stored in

> **Plain Text and HTML attachments**
>
> If you attach a file to a message in Plain Text or HTML format, the attachment appears in a separate pane at the bottom of the message window, instead of as part of the message.

your Outbox. You also want to check whether you have any mail. Here's how to send and retrieve messages:

Send/Receive

The Send/Receive button

1. Click the Standard toolbar's More Buttons button, and then, on the drop-down palette, click the Send/Receive button. (If Outlook is set up for more than one e-mail service, choose Send/Receive from the Tools menu and then choose either the service you want or All Accounts.) Outlook tells you it is checking for new messages and sending outgoing messages. (Internet e-mail users may have to enter a user name and password first.)

New message alert

When Outlook is finished, it displays the number of new messages in parentheses next to the Inbox icon on the Outlook bar and displays an envelope icon in the status bar. It may also sound an alert to announce the arrival of the messages, and it may disconnect you from your e-mail server.

Whether you are permanently connected to your e-mail server or you had to manually retrieve your messages, the message header pane now looks like this:

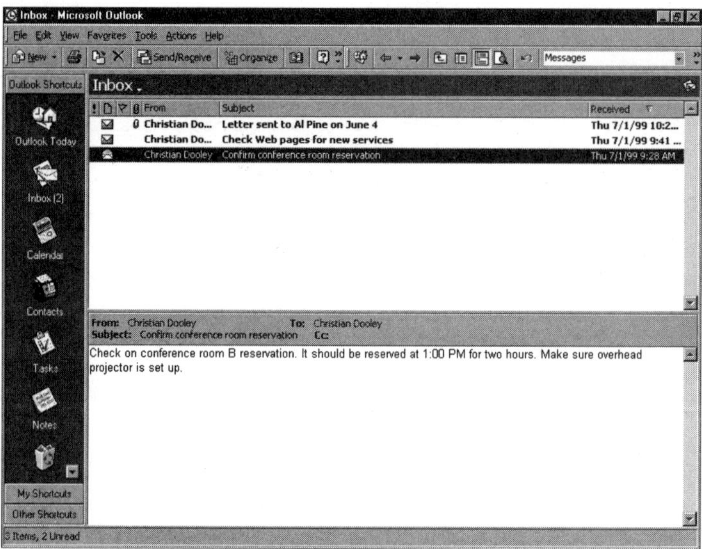

Until you read a message, its header is displayed in bold type. Icons on the left tell you more about the message (see the adjacent tip). Let's read a message right now:

Inbox message symbols

The first column of the Inbox window displays an exclamation mark if the sender has indicated that the message is of high priority. A down arrow indicates that a message is of low priority. (For more information, see the tip on page 65.) The second column of the Inbox window displays symbols indicating the status of each message. The most common symbols show whether the message has been read—an open envelope—or not read—a closed envelope. (For a detailed listing of the other symbols, look up *symbol* in the Help feature.) The third column displays a flag icon if the message has been flagged. (See the tip on page 71.) The fourth column displays a paper clip icon if the message has an attachment.

1. Click the header of the message with the attachment (the one with the paper clip—see the tip on the facing page) to display its contents in the preview pane below.
2. Now double-click the same message header to display it in a window, like this:

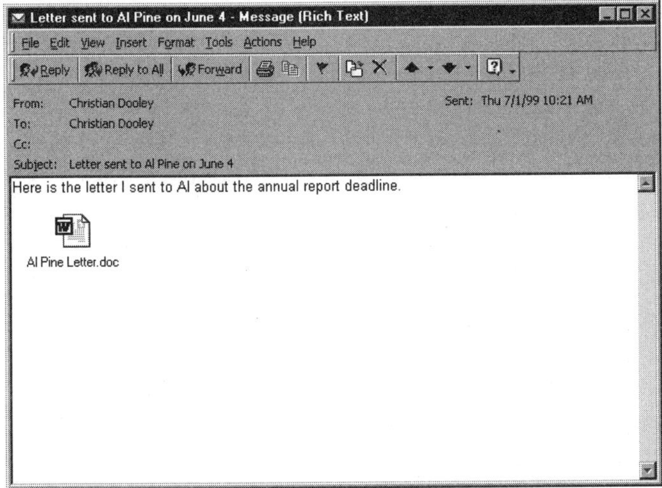

3. To read the attachment, just double-click it. The dialog box shown on the next page may appear.

Flagging messages

Flagging messages calls attention to them and indicates that an action needs to be taken. You can flag messages you have received as well as messages you send. To flag a received message so that you can remind yourself to do something with it, simply right-click the message and choose Flag For Follow Up from the shortcut menu. In the Flag To edit box, select an action that needs to be taken, such as Call or Reply. In the Due By edit box, you can specify the date by which you want to complete the follow-up task. To flag an outgoing message, choose Flag For Follow Up from the Actions menu in the Message window. Then fill in the Flag To and Due By edit boxes as necessary and click OK. When the recipient receives the message, Outlook displays the flag symbol next to the message header. When the message is opened in its own window, Outlook displays what type of action is requested at the top of the message. To indicate that you have taken care of the task, you can right-click the message and choose Flag Complete from the shortcut menu to change the flag's color to white, or choose Clear Flag to remove the flag icon.

Marking messages

When you select an unread message header, Outlook removes the bold formatting after a few seconds because it assumes you have read the message in the preview pane. You can manually make this change by choosing Mark As Read or Mark All As Read from the Edit menu. You can also choose Mark As Unread to make a message header stand out. To display only the unread messages (both those you have really not read and those you have marked as unread), choose Current View and then Unread Messages from the View menu.

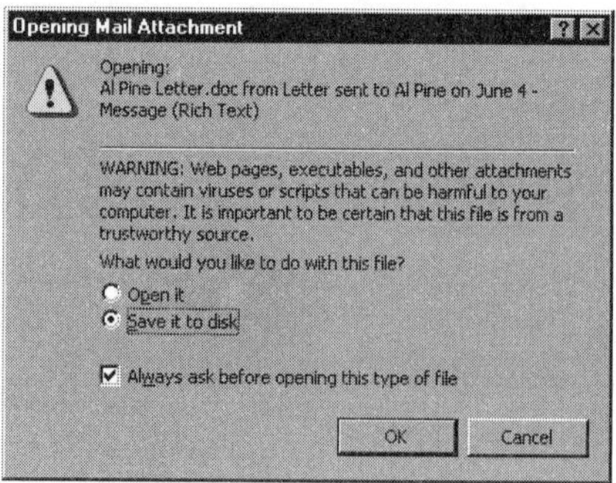

4. Because you know this file came from a safe place (your own hard drive), click the Open It option and then click OK to open the attachment in the program in which it was created. Then close the program to return to Outlook. (See the tip below for more information about handling attachments from other locations.)

Replying to Messages

Suppose this message is from a colleague and requires a response. Follow these steps to send a reply:

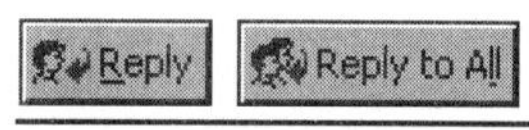

The Reply and the Reply To All buttons

1. Click the Reply button. (To send the response to the sender of the message and to all recipients of courtesy copies, you would click the Reply To All button.) Outlook opens a Message window like this one:

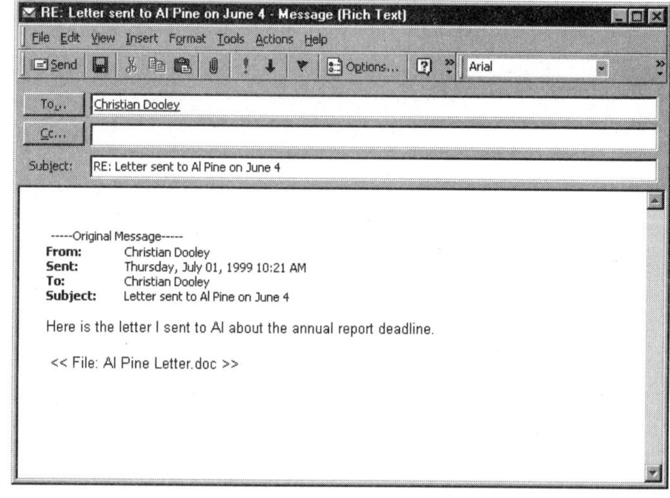

Scanning for viruses

When you receive a message with an attachment, save the attachment in a temporary folder and scan the folder for viruses before you do anything with the file. You can't "catch" a virus by just looking at a file, but activating a file infected with a virus can wreak havoc. Although viruses usually do their damage via program files, new breeds of viruses attack word processor and spreadsheet files. So get in the habit of scanning *all* attachment files with a virus program unless you are sure the files are coming from an impeccable source.

Notice that the To and Subject edit boxes are already filled in. Also notice that the original message appears below the blinking insertion point. (If you prefer not to display the original message in your responses, read the tip below.) The attachment appears in chevrons to indicate that it will not be sent as part of the reply.

2. Type *Thanks for the letter. That should work!* Then click the Send button. Back in the original Message window, Outlook has added a note that you have sent a reply to this message.

Forwarding Messages

If you receive a message that you think will be of interest to a colleague, you can easily forward the message with just a few mouse clicks. Follow these steps to try it:

1. With the Letter Sent To Al Pine message still displayed in its window, click the Forward button on the toolbar to display the Message window shown here:

The Forward button

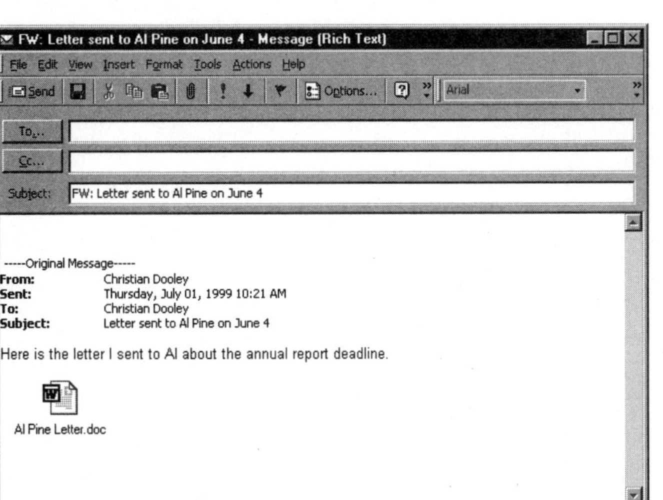

This time only the Subject edit box is filled in. Again, the original message appears below the insertion point, but the attachment icon is intact, indicating that the attachment will be sent as part of the forwarded message.

2. For demonstration purposes, type your own e-mail address in the To box and click the Send button. Outlook changes the

No original message in replies

If you don't want Outlook to display the original message at the end of your reply, choose Options from Outlook's Tools menu and click the E-mail Options button on the Preferences tab. Click the arrow to the right of the When Replying To A Message box, select Do Not Include Original Message, and click OK twice. (Notice that you can also change the way the original message appears within a forwarded message using this dialog box.)

note in the original Message window to indicate that you forwarded the message.

3. To view the two new messages, close the Message window and if necessary, click the Send/Receive button. The header pane now looks like this:

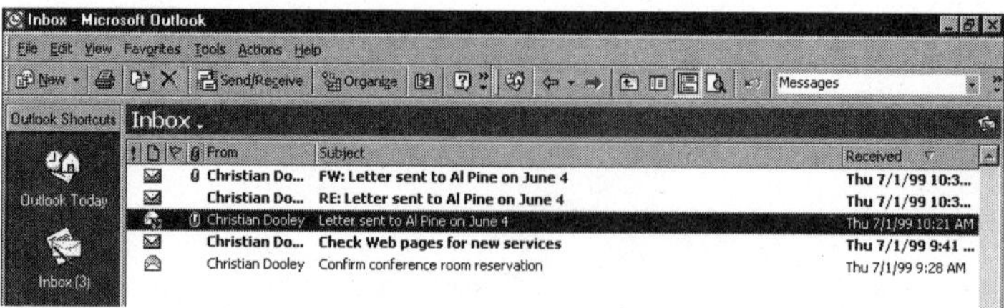

The arrow on the envelope icon of the original Al Pine message tells you that you have forwarded this message.

4. Open both new messages to check them out.

Deleting Messages

In the early days of e-mail, people would often hold onto old e-mail messages so that they had a record of their senders' addresses. Because it is so easy to add e-mail addresses to the contact list, this reason for keeping old messages no longer exists, and after you have read most of your messages, you will probably want to delete them. To demonstrate how to delete messages, you'll clean up the Sent Items folder, but bear in mind that the procedure is the same for any Outlook e-mail folder. Follow the steps at the top of the facing page.

Saving messages and attachments

To save a message for use in another program, select the message in the Inbox window, choose Save As from the File menu, navigate to the desired storage location, name the file, designate the file type, and click Save. You can save e-mail messages as RTF (RichText Format), Text Only, Outlook Template, or Message Format. (The Outlook Template file type allows you to use the file as a template for other Outlook messages. The Message Format file type is associated with Outlook, which opens the file if you double-click its filename.) To save an attachment to an e-mail message as a separate file, open the message, choose Save Attachments from the File menu, select the attachment's filename, and then designate the storage location for the file. (You can also right-click the attachment icon and choose Save As from the shortcut menu; or you can click the paper clip icon at the right end of the preview pane's title bar, select the file to open it in the appropriate application, and then save it in the usual way.) To save an attachment without opening the message, simply select the message header in the workspace and choose Save Attachments from the File menu.

1. Click the My Shortcuts button and then click the Sent Items icon on the Outlook bar to display a listing in the workspace of all the messages you have sent, as shown here:

The Sent Items icon

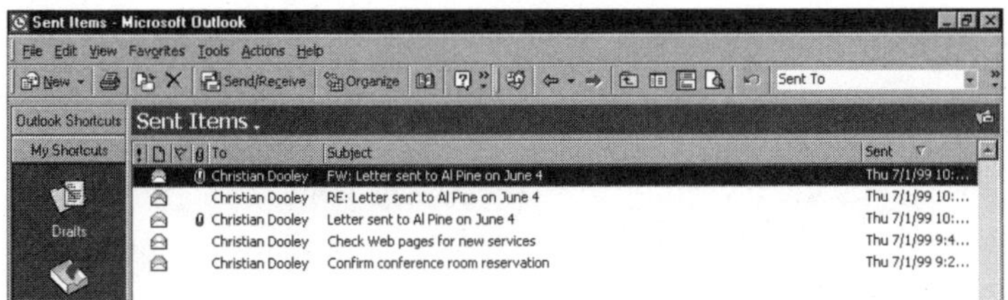

2. Choose Select All from the Edit menu and then click the Delete button on the toolbar. Instead of actually deleting the messages, Outlook transfers them to the Deleted Items folder, giving you another opportunity to change your mind about getting rid of them.

3. Click the Outlook Shortcuts button and then click the Deleted Items icon on the Outlook bar to display that folder's contents.

The Deleted Items icon

4. You really do want to delete these files, so choose Empty "Deleted Items" Folder from the Tools menu. Click Yes when asked whether you want to get rid of the items for good.

5. Display the contents of the Inbox and delete any messages you don't need. Be sure to keep the five messages you have sent to yourself.

If you want to permanently delete messages without having to later deal with them in the Deleted Items folder, you can choose Options from the Tools menu and select the Empty The Deleted Items Folder Upon Exiting check box in the General section of the Other tab. Then Outlook erases the folder's contents every time you exit the program.

Don't save sent messages

To keep your Outlook files from growing too big, you can turn off the option that automatically saves a copy of all your outgoing messages in the Sent Items folder. Choose Options from the Tools menu and click the E-mail Options button on the Preferences tab. Deselect the Save Copies Of Messages In Sent Items Folder check box in the Message Handling section, and click OK twice. If you later want to save a particular outgoing message in the Sent Items folder, click the Options button in the Message window before you send the message, select the Save Sent Message To check box, designate a location, and click Close.

Organizing Messages

If you start sending and receiving lots of e-mail messages that you need to keep, you will want to organize the Inbox so specific messages are easier to find. As with the Notes and Contacts components, you can change the way you view messages, either by using one of Outlook's predefined views or by creating a view of your own. You can also create folders to supplement the default e-mail folders. For the remainder of this chapter, you will look at ways to keep the messages you send and receive in a more logical order.

Switching Views

So far, you have worked with the Inbox using the default messages view. Let's quickly take a look at some of the other available views:

1. Click the arrow to the right of the Current View box on the Advanced toolbar and select By Conversation Topic from the drop-down list, or choose Current View and By Conversation Topic from the View menu. The contents of the Inbox now look something like this:

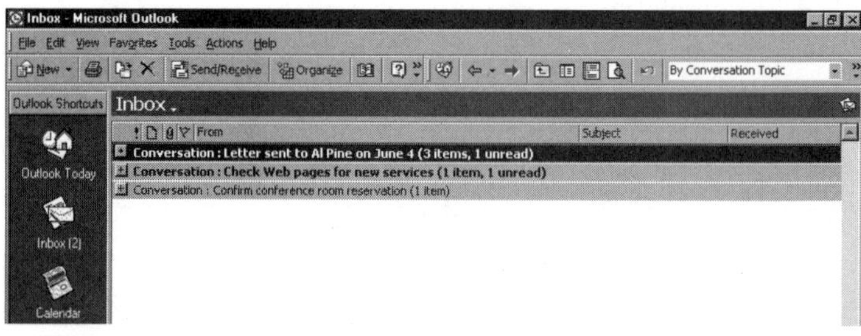

Outlook organizes the messages by topic and displays a plus sign next to each one. When you click the plus sign, Outlook displays all messages about that topic in date/time order, with the most recent message first.

2. Click the plus sign next to the first topic to display all its messages, and then click the minus sign to collapse the list again.
3. Now change the Current View box's setting to Unread Messages. In this view, Outlook displays only the messages you have not yet read. (If you have read all of them, then the window is blank.)
4. Experiment with some of the other available views and then return to the original view by selecting Messages from the Current View drop-down list.

Recalling messages

If you are working on a network that uses Exchange Server, you can recall or replace e-mail messages you have recently sent to a coworker. First display the Sent Items folder and open the message you want to recall. Choose Recall This Message from the Actions menu, select Delete Unread Copies Of This Message, and click OK. To replace the message with a new one, select the second option in the Recall This Message dialog box, click OK, and type a new message. If you want to be notified about the recall or replacement of the message, click the Tell Me check box. (Bear in mind that this feature only works if the recipient has not yet opened or moved the message you want to recall.)

Applying Custom Filters

In the previous section, Outlook displayed only unread messages by applying a filter to the list of messages. Filters can help you find a particular message by allowing you to temporarily focus on a subset of the information in the message list. When you want to find a specific message, you can create your own filter. Let's look for the message that you received some time during the last seven days about a letter to Al Pine:

1. Choose Current View and then Customize Current View from the View menu to display the View Summary dialog box shown earlier on page 21.
2. Click the Filter button to display this dialog box:

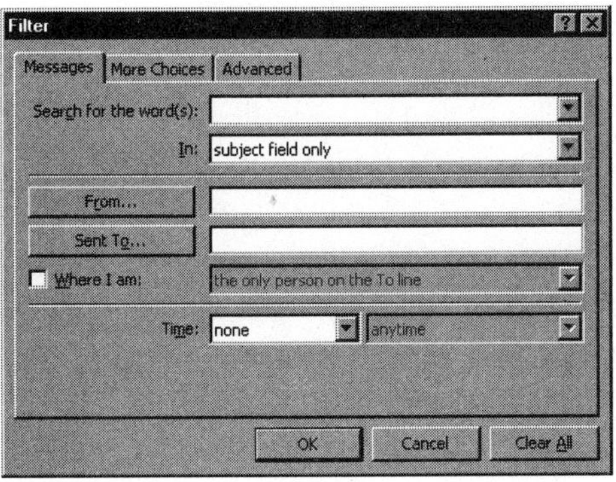

3. On the Messages tab, type *letter* in the Search For The Word(s) edit box.
4. Check that Subject Field Only is selected in the In edit box to limit the search to the Subject lines of the messages in the Inbox, and then type your name in the From box.
5. Click the arrow to the right of the Time box and select Received. Then click the arrow in the box to the right and select In The Last 7 Days.
6. Click OK twice. Outlook filters the message list according to your criteria and displays the results in the workspace as shown on the next page.

More about filters

If you receive tons of messages and need to search for a particular one, you may want to experiment with the other tabs in the Filter dialog box. On the More Choices tab, you can create a filter that looks for messages assigned to a particular category. You can also search for messages that have or have not been read, messages that have or don't have attachments, and messages that have a designated importance level. On the Advanced tab, you can set up more specific filtering criteria by clicking the Field button, selecting a message field from the drop-down list, and then specifying a condition that the field must meet by selecting an item from the Condition box. Next type a value for the field in the Value edit box, and then click Add To List to add this criteria to any others you have created. When you click OK twice, Outlook filters your message list and displays only those messages that meet the criteria specified in the Filter dialog box.

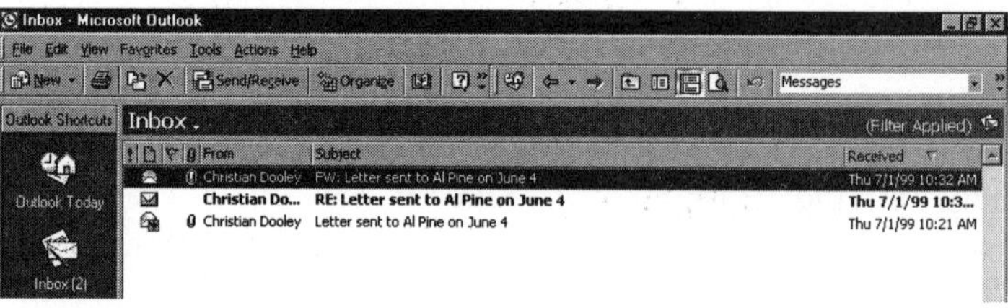

Notice that Outlook displays *(Filter Applied)* at the right end of the workspace title bar to remind you that you are not looking at the complete list of messages.

Removing a filter

7. To redisplay the entire message list, right-click a column header and choose Customize Current View from the shortcut menu. Click the Filter button, click Clear All, and then click OK twice.

Using Folders

Switching views and customizing them with filters are two useful ways to organize e-mail. But if you work on many projects simultaneously, you may find that you want to store your e-mail by project. By creating folders to store messages, you can categorize them and keep them better organized. As an example, suppose that at Ferguson and Bardell, you might deal with both coworkers and clients. Let's create folders for these two categories now:

1. With the Inbox active, choose Folder and then New Folder from the File menu to display this dialog box:

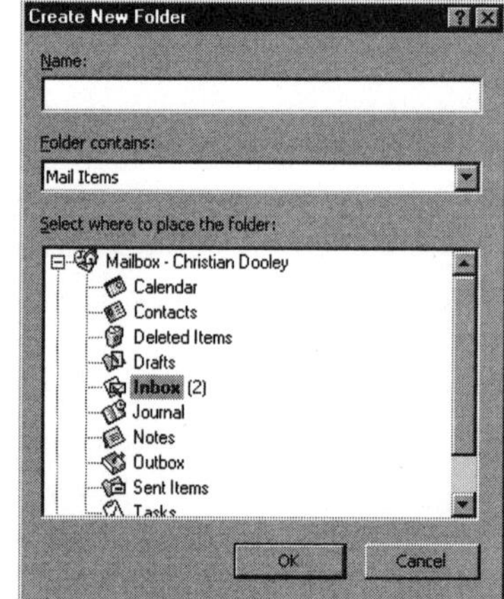

Filtering junk e-mail

Some businesses and organizations send mass mailings via e-mail just as they do via regular mail. If you don't want to receive junk e-mail, you can tell Outlook to automatically move it to a folder other than the Inbox or to color-code it. With the Inbox displayed, click the Organize button on the toolbar. Click the Junk E-Mail option and then select the desired options from the adjacent drop-down lists. After you make your selections, click the Turn On buttons. To designate a specific address as junk e-mail, right-click the message header and choose Junk E-Mail and then Add To Junk Senders List from the shortcut menu. (You can filter e-mail messages with adult content in the same way.)

2. Type *Coworkers* in the Name box and click OK.

3. When asked whether you want to add an icon for this folder to the Outlook bar, click Yes.

4. The My Shortcuts button is flashing on the Outlook bar. Click the button to open the My Shortcuts group, which now includes an icon for the Coworkers folder.

5. Repeat steps 1 through 3 to create a folder called *Clients* with an icon in the My Shortcuts group.

To see all the folders that you can access from the shortcuts on the Outlook bar, you can display the folders as a hierarchical list. Follow these steps:

The Folder List button

1. Click the Folder List button on the Advanced toolbar, or choose Folder List from the View menu. The Outlook window now looks like this:

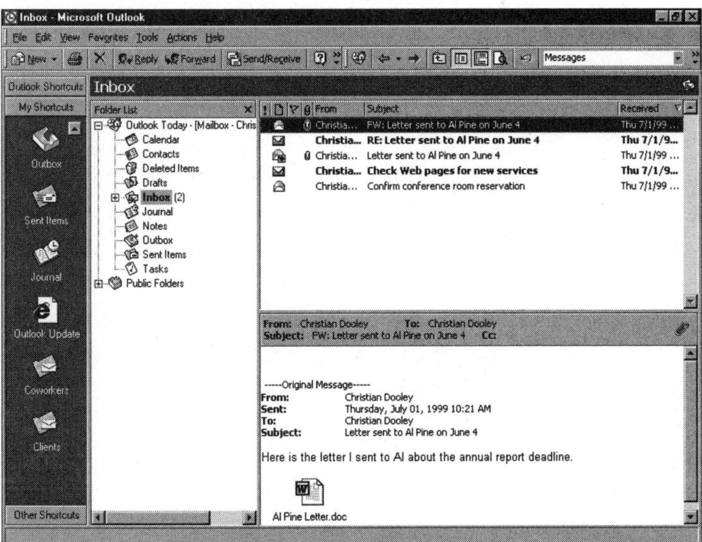

As you can see, the folder list is sandwiched between the Outlook bar and the workspace.

2. In the list, click the plus sign next to the Inbox folder to display the folders you just created.

3. To display only the folder list, choose Outlook Bar from the View menu to turn it off.

Moving Messages

You have created a couple of folders in which to place your messages, so now you need to move the messages into the appropriate storage locations. Follow these steps:

Selecting more than one message at a time

1. With the Inbox folder selected in the folder list and its contents displayed in the workspace, select both the reply and the forwarded message about the letter to Al Pine by selecting one, holding down the Shift key, and selecting the other.
2. With the messages highlighted, drag them to the Clients folder. When you release the mouse button, Outlook moves the messages from the Inbox folder to the Clients folder.
3. Move the Confirm Conference Room message from the Inbox folder to the Coworkers folder.

Closing the folder list

4. Next click the Folder List's Close button to close it and then choose Outlook Bar from the View menu to redisplay the Outlook bar.
5. In the My Shortcuts group on the Outlook bar, click first the Coworkers icon and then the Clients icon to view their contents in the workspace.

Organizing Messages with the Rules Wizard

If your correspondence falls into identifiable categories that you usually want to handle in specific ways, you can enlist the help of the Rules Wizard in automating the organization of your e-mail. As a simple example, let's set up a rule that tells Outlook to move all messages concerning Al Pine into the Clients folder. Follow these steps:

The Rules Wizard button

1. Click the Rules Wizard button on the Advanced toolbar, or choose Rules Wizard from the Tools menu. Then in the Rules Wizard dialog box, click New to start the wizard, which displays the dialog box shown at the top of the facing page.

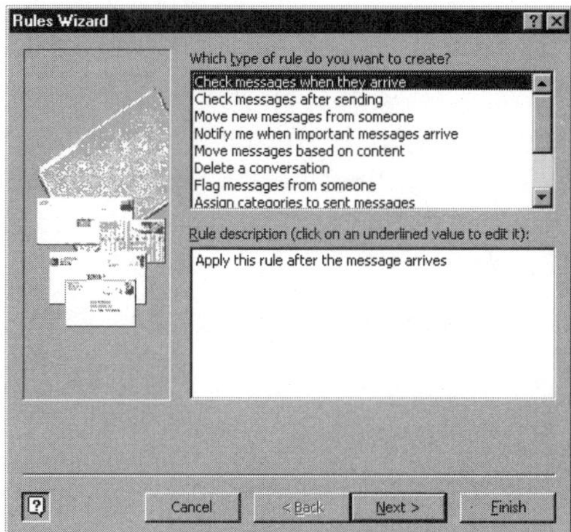

2. Select Move Messages Based On Content and click Next:

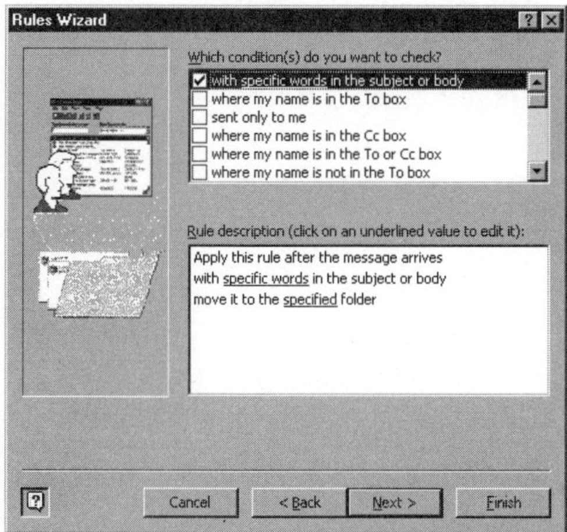

3. Leave With Specific Words In The Subject Or Body selected, select Where My Name Is In The To Or Cc Box, and click specific words in the box below to display this dialog box:

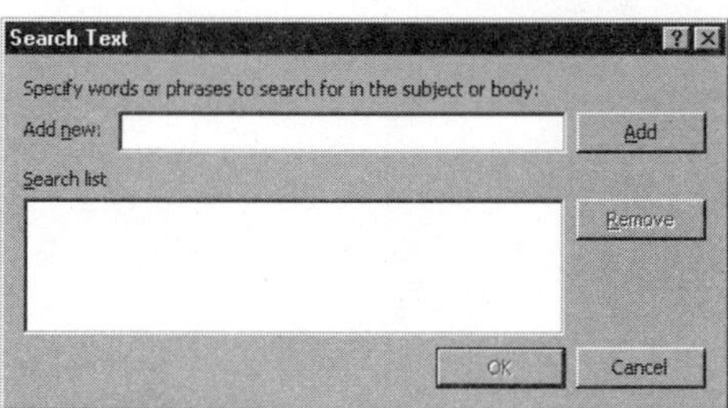

4. Type *Al Pine* in the Add New edit box, click Add, and then click OK. Back in the wizard's dialog box, click the word specified in the Rule Description box, display the two Inbox subfolders in the folder list by clicking the plus sign, and double-click Clients. Then click Next to show this dialog box:

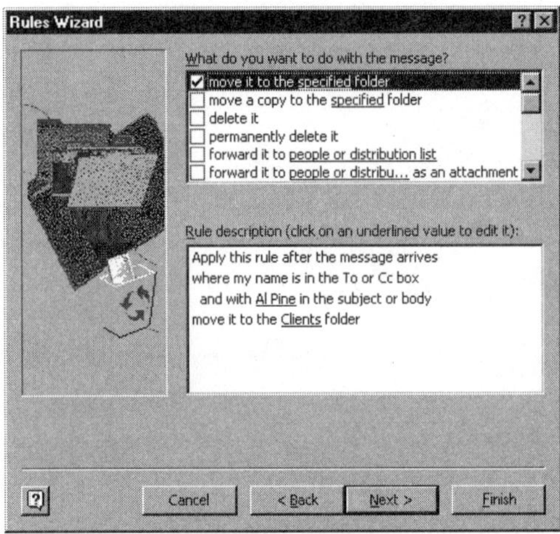

5. Click Next to confirm that you want to move Al Pine messages to the Clients folder. When you see a dialog box where you can specify exceptions to the rule, click Next again.

6. Type *Al Pine* as the name for the rule, and with Turn On This Rule selected, click Finish to close the wizard. The rule is now listed in the Rules Wizard dialog box, as shown here:

7. Click the Run Now button to display the Run Rules Now dialog box. Select the Al Pine rule. If the Run In Folder setting is not Inbox, click the Browse button, click Inbox, and click OK. Then click Run Now. After Outlook moves the original message about the letter to Al Pine to the Clients folder, click Close and then OK to close the open dialog boxes.

Now let's test the rule:

1. Write a new message to yourself about a meeting with Al Pine, and then send it by clicking the Send button. If necessary, click the Send/Receive button to deliver the message to your Inbox. Outlook applies the Al Pine rule to the new message and automatically moves it to the Clients folder.
2. Display the contents of the Clients folder in the workspace so that you can confirm that the rule works.

If you set up several rules like this one, you might find that having to check several folders for new messages instead of one decreases your efficiency rather than increases it. In that case, you can display the Rules Wizard dialog box, select a rule, click Options, and change the Update setting to Manually. Then after you have read new messages in the Inbox, you can click the Run Now button in the Rules Wizard dialog box to have Outlook organize the messages.

Manually applying a rule

Well, that wraps up our discussion of the e-mail component of Outlook. Keeping your messages organized efficiently is bound to make you more productive, so we encourage you to experiment with the organization features discussed in this and the other chapters.

4 Managing Your Schedule

In this chapter, we show you how to use Outlook's Calendar component to manage your time. You schedule appointments, set up a recurring appointment, and allocate time for longer events. Then you see how to plan meetings and send meeting requests to attendees.

The appointments you schedule represent those normally associated with a work environment. However, you can also use Calendar to organize and manage the schedule of a club, a school group, or your family.

Tasks performed and concepts covered:

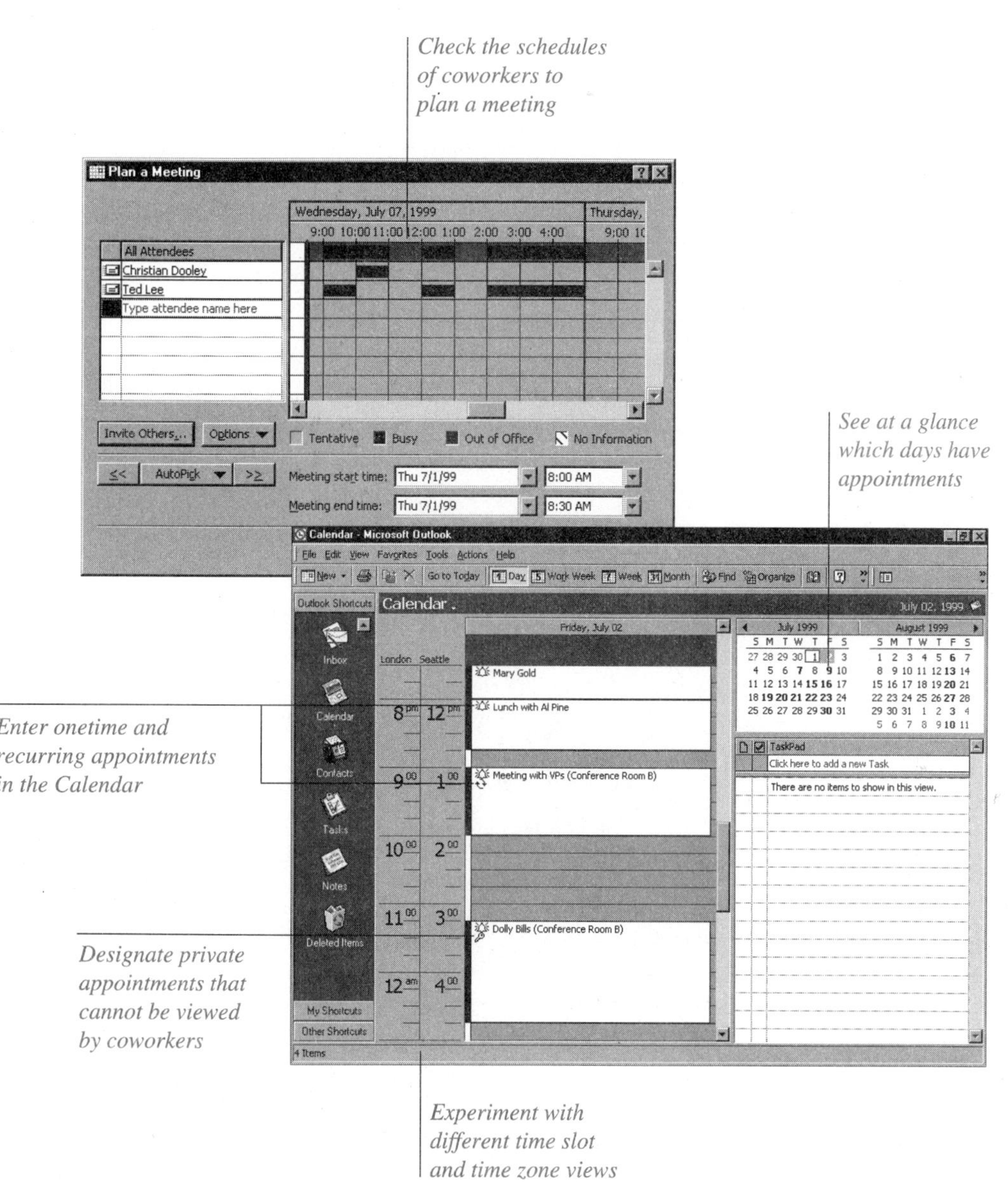

The Calendar component of Outlook is designed to take the hassle out of time management by enabling you to keep track of appointments. If used faithfully, Calendar can eliminate the need for a paper calendar and can actually function better than one. With Calendar, you can create detailed appointments, set recurring appointments, plan meetings, and ask to be reminded of these commitments ahead of time.

Outlook's Calendar component is most useful to you when you keep Outlook running throughout the workday. Some of its features are available only if you are working on a network where Microsoft Exchange Server handles internal communications. In this chapter, you'll explore all of Calendar's useful features. If your computer is not hooked up to a network that uses Exchange Server, you can skip the sections that don't apply for your computer's setup. Let's take a look at Calendar:

1. If necessary, start Outlook.

The Calendar icon

2. Click the Calendar icon on the Outlook bar. The workspace now looks like this:

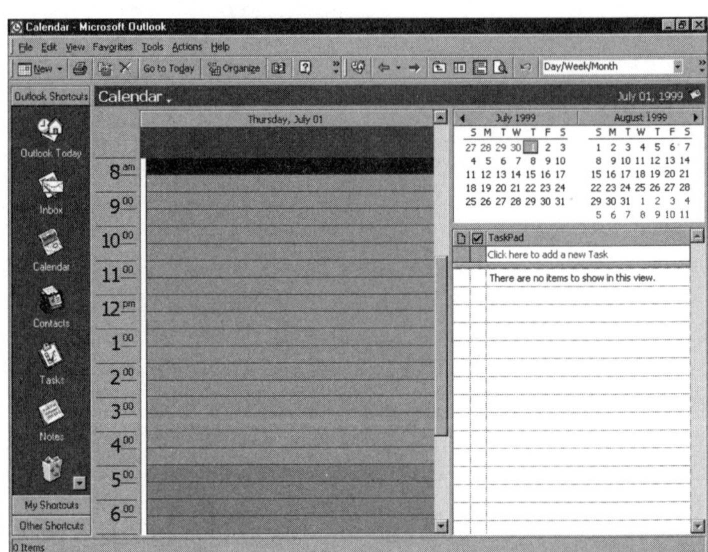

On the left side is the *appointment pane*, divided into half-hour intervals. By default, Outlook displays your schedule for

Computer dating

Outlook obtains the date and time from your system clock. If this clock is wrong, Outlook keeps an inaccurate calendar and reminds you of appointments at the wrong time. To set the right date and time, double-click the clock at the right end of the Windows taskbar. In the Date/Time Properties dialog box, make the appropriate adjustments to the date or time. If Outlook has trouble keeping your schedule, there may be problems with your computer's battery, which maintains the system clock.

today. In the top right corner is the date navigator, which displays calendars for the current month and next month. (You can cycle through the months by clicking the left and right arrows on the calendar headers.) In the bottom right corner is a small version of the to-do list maintained by the Tasks component, called the *TaskPad*. (We discuss Tasks and the to-do list in Chapter 5.)

The TaskPad

Scheduling Appointments

The half-hour intervals in the appointment pane designate time slots. You use these time slots to schedule appointments for the day. Suppose you have a meeting with Al Pine at 3:00 this afternoon, which you expect to last half an hour. Here's how easy it is to enter the appointment:

1. Click the 3:00 time slot, type *Al Pine*, and press Enter. (If it is now later than 3:00 PM, pick a later time. You can enter an appointment that has already occurred, but Outlook can't remind you about it.)

Entering appointments in the appointment pane

That's all there is to it. The Al Pine appointment now occupies the 3:00 slot, and a bell icon tells you that Outlook will remind you of the appointment 15 minutes in advance. Today's date is now bold in the date navigator, indicating that you have an appointment today.

Now suppose you need to schedule an interview with a prospective new financial analyst named Dolly Bills at 4:15 PM tomorrow. The interview will probably last an hour and a half. Follow these steps:

1. Click tomorrow's date in the date navigator. Tomorrow's appointment area is now displayed.
2. Because the time slots are in half-hour intervals, you need to make a special entry for Dolly Bills. Double-click the 4:00 time slot to display the Appointment window shown at the top of the following page, in which you can tailor your appointments.

Other ways to enter appointments

Another way to add an appointment to your schedule is to select the complete time of the appointment with the mouse, right-click the selection, and then choose New Appointment from the shortcut menu. Outlook then displays the Appointment window with the start and end times already filled in. If you don't want to type appointments directly in the appointment pane, you can click the New button on the toolbar or choose New and then Appointment from the File menu to display the Appointment window.

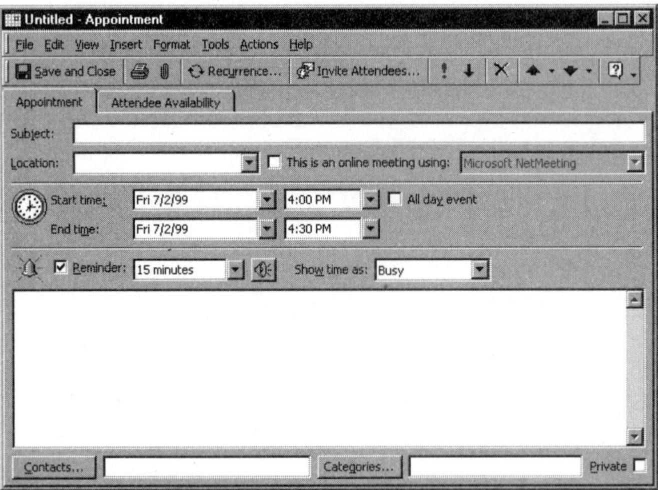

3. In the Subject edit box, type *Dolly Bills*, and in the Location edit box, type *Conference Room B*. (You can also click the arrow to the right of the Location edit box to select from a drop-down list of the last seven locations you have used.)

Tailoring the start time

4. Change the start time by selecting 00 in 4:00 PM and typing *15*. Then change the end time to 5:45 PM by clicking the End Time edit box, clicking its arrow, and selecting 5:45 from the drop-down list.

Creating appointments from messages

You can schedule appointments based on e-mail messages you have received. Select the desired message header in the Inbox and drag it to the Calendar icon on the Outlook bar. Outlook then displays the Appointment window with the contents of the message displayed in the message area at the bottom of the window and with the message subject displayed in the Subject edit box. To complete the appointment, fill in the remaining information and then click Save And Close.

5. Change the Reminder time to 10 Minutes by either typing the time or selecting it from the drop-down list.

6. Click the arrow to the right of the Show Time As edit box to display a drop-down list of four options: Free, Tentative, Busy, and Out Of Office. If you are working on a network that uses Exchange Server, these four options show anyone who is trying to set up a meeting whether or not you are available at this time. Selecting Tentative or Free displays the time in a light color on other people's computers and indicates that you might be available. Selecting Busy or Out Of Office displays the time in a dark color and indicates that you are not available.

7. Leave the Busy option selected by clicking away from the list, and then click the Private check box in the bottom right corner

of the window. (Other people will see that you are not available at this time, but they will not be able to see why.)

8. Click Save And Close to confirm the appointment. The appointment pane now looks like this:

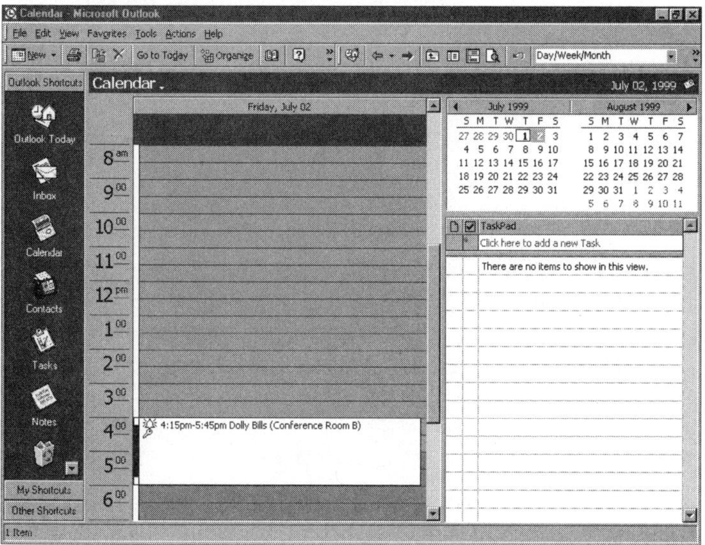

9. Click the Go To Today button on the toolbar or click today's date in the date navigator to move back to the appointment pane for today.

When the reminder time for an appointment arrives, you see this message box:

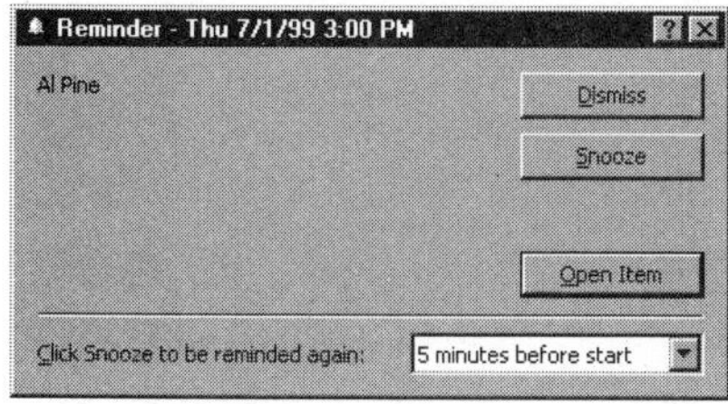

(If the Office Assistant is turned on, it displays the message instead.) You can click the Dismiss button to tell Outlook not to remind you again about this appointment; you can click the Snooze button to be reminded again in the period

Changing workday default times

By default, Outlook uses an 8:00 AM to 5:00 PM, Monday through Friday workweek and displays these hours in the appointment pane in a light color, with all other hours of the day in a darker shade. But if your schedule is different, you can change the default times and days. Choose Options from the Tools menu and click the Calendar Options button on the Preferences tab. In the Calendar Work Week section, enter the start and end times of your workday. To change the days worked, click the desired days' check boxes. Then click OK twice.

designated at the bottom of the message box; or you can click the Open Item button to display the Appointment window to refresh your memory about the details of the appointment.

Scheduling Recurring Appointments

Unless you specify otherwise, the appointments you schedule are onetime occurrences. You can designate appointments that occur at the same time at regular intervals as *recurring*. Then instead of having to enter the appointment manually over and over again, you can let Outlook automatically make that appointment for you.

Attaching files to appointments

If a file is associated with an appointment you have scheduled, you can attach the file to the appointment—for example, to remind you to print it beforehand. After scheduling the appointment in the Appointment window, click an insertion point in the message area at the bottom of the window and click the Insert File button on the toolbar. Outlook displays the Insert File dialog box shown on page 69, where you navigate to the file you want to attach and select it. You can then specify how you want the file inserted by clicking the arrow to the right of the Insert button and selecting an option from the drop-down list. If you insert the file as text, the file becomes part of the appointment. If you insert the file as an attachment, Outlook attaches a copy of the file to the appointment as an icon. If you insert the file as a shortcut, Outlook adds a shortcut to the appointment that you can simply double-click to open the original file.

For example, suppose you meet with a group of senior consultants every other Wednesday from 10:00 to 11:00 AM. Here's how to schedule this recurring appointment:

1. Click next Wednesday's date in the date navigator and drag through the time slots for 10:00 and 10:30 to select them.
2. Choose New Recurring Appointment from the Actions menu. Outlook opens an Appointment window and then displays this dialog box:

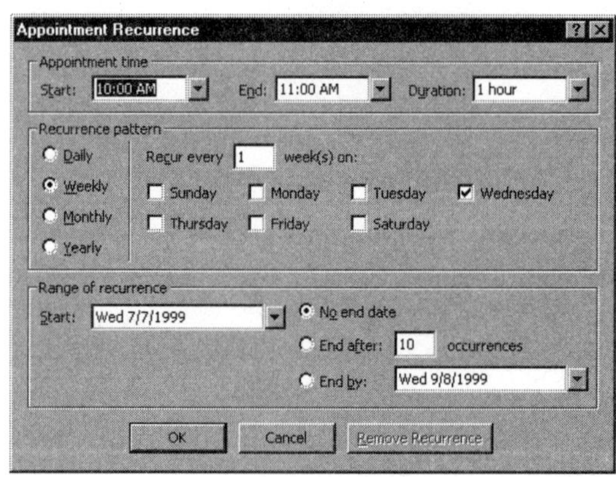

By default, Outlook assumes you want the meeting to occur weekly on the same day of the week, starting and ending at the times you selected, with no end date.

3. In the Recurrence Pattern section, enter *2* in the Recur Every edit box to change the appointment to every other week.

4. To add an end date, click the End By option in the Range Of Recurrence section and use the drop-down calendar to change the date to the last Wednesday of the year. Then click OK.

Specifying an end date for a recurring appointment

5. In the Appointment window, type *Client Status Report* in the Subject edit box. Click the arrow to the right of the Location edit box and select Conference Room B, change the reminder time for the appointment to 30 Minutes, and then click Save And Close. The result is shown here:

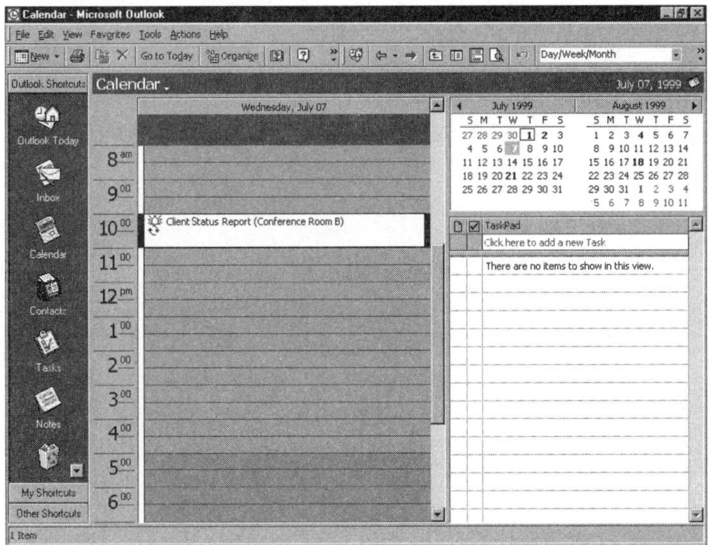

Outlook has entered the recurring appointment in the specified time slot for next Wednesday and also for every other Wednesday thereafter, designating it with circular arrows to indicate that the appointment is recurring.

Scheduling Events

Sometimes appointments last for an entire day or even longer. Outlook refers to these long appointments as events. For example, you might need to schedule a day-long presentation at a client's office or attend a week-long conference in another city. Scheduling events is similar to scheduling regular appointments. Here's what you do:

1. Click a date two weeks from now on the date navigator, and double-click the blank space at the top of the appointment

Problems with the Every Weekday option?

If you altered your workday settings (see the tip on page 89), Outlook doesn't record recurring appointments correctly when you use the Every Weekday option in the Recurrence Pattern section of the Appointment Recurrence dialog box. (This option becomes available after you click the Daily option.) For example, if you have set your workdays to Tuesday through Saturday and then you create a recurring appointment for every weekday, Outlook schedules the appointment for the default Monday through Friday weekdays. To work around this problem, use the Weekly option instead of the Every Weekday option and select the check boxes for the desired days.

pane to tell Outlook that you want to enter an event. Outlook displays this Event window:

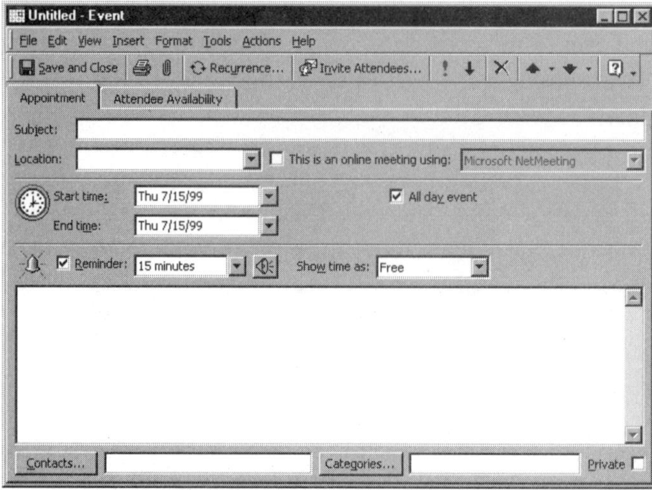

2. Type *Annual Report Presentation* in the Subject edit box, then type *Cream of the Crop Corporate Office* in the Location edit box, change the Reminder setting to 0.5 Days, and change the Show Time As option to Out Of Office. Notice that Outlook has selected the All Day Event check box.

3. Click Save And Close. The appointment pane looks like this:

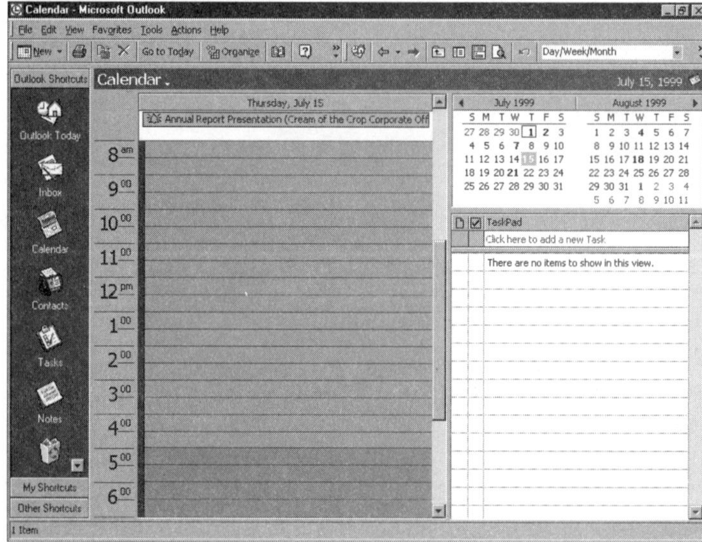

Making existing appointments recur

To turn an existing appointment into a recurring one, double-click the appointment in the appointment pane and click the Recurrence button. Outlook displays the Appointment Recurrence dialog box, where you can select the recurrence options you want. When you finish, click OK and then click Save And Close.

Now suppose you want to enter a week-long event for a conference you will attend in Boston. Follow these steps:

Entering week-long events

1. First click the Monday following the presentation at Cream of the Crop in the date navigator, and then choose New All Day Event from the Actions menu. Outlook displays the Event window.

2. Type *Boston Financial Conference* in the Subject edit box, type *Charles River Convention Center* in the Location edit box, deselect the Reminder check box, and change the Show Time As option to Out Of Office.

3. Click the arrow to the right of the End Time edit box and block out the entire week by selecting the Friday of the week you have chosen. Outlook displays a warning message at the top of the window stating that you already have another appointment entered during this time (the recurring senior consultant's meeting).

4. Go ahead and click Save And Close.

5. Notice in the date navigator that the entire week is now marked in bold. Click one or two of the dates in the designated week to check that Outlook has entered the conference correctly.

Scheduling recurring events

Like appointments, events can occur regularly at weekly, monthly, or yearly intervals. For example, if you always have a day-long meeting at a client's office on the last Friday of every month, or if your office always closes the day after Thanksgiving, you can mark these recurring events throughout your calendar. Choose New All Day Event from the Actions menu to display the Appointment window, and then click the Recurrence button. Notice that the start and end times are set to Midnight, designating the appointment as an all day event. Fill in the information as you would with any other appointment, click OK, and then click Save And Close. Bear in mind that when you enter recurring events such as birthdays and anniversaries in a contact's address card, the event is automatically added to the calendar. (See page 40 for more information.)

Editing Appointments

Sometimes you will need to change an appointment to either fix errors or update details. Usually, you can double-click the appointment to open its Appointment window and then edit the appropriate area, but for certain changes you can take shortcuts. Let's try some shortcuts now as you change the appointment time for the interview with Dolly Bills:

1. First display the calendar for the day on which you entered Dolly Bill's interview appointment.

2. Point to the border on the left side of the appointment. When the pointer turns into a four-headed arrow, hold down the left mouse button and drag upward to the 3:00 PM time slot.

3. When the top of the appointment box is even with the 3:00 PM time slot, release the mouse button. Outlook moves the appointment and adjusts the times displayed in the box to reflect the fact that the appointment starts at the quarter-hour, as shown here:

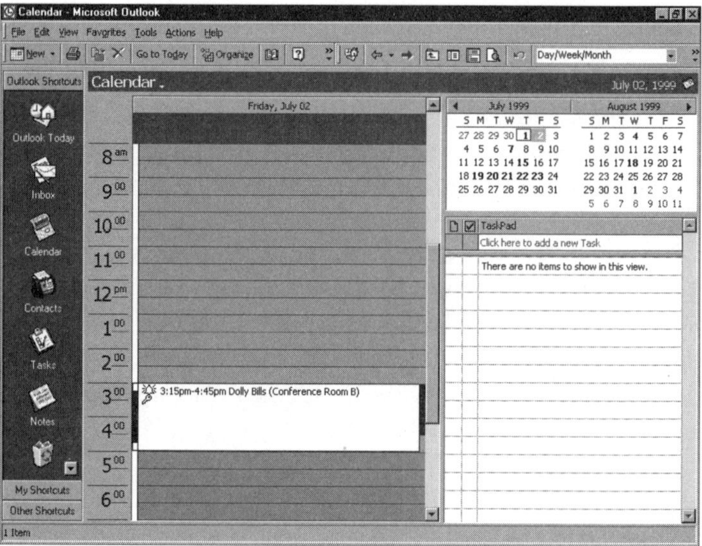

Adding holidays

If you work with clients or customers in other countries, you may want to track the national holidays of those countries in Calendar. To do so, choose Options from the Tools menu, click Calendar Options on the Preferences tab, and then click the Add Holidays button. You can then select the holidays of various countries as well as those of certain religions to add them to your calendar. If you want to remove a holiday or holidays, choose Current View and then Events from the view menu, select the holidays you want to remove, and click the Delete button.

Now suppose you need to allow an additional half-hour for Al Pine's appointment. Here's how to change the appointment in the appointment pane:

1. Display the Al Pine appointment and point to the bottom border of its time slot.
2. When the pointer turns into a double-headed arrow, drag downward through the 3:30 PM time slot, release the mouse button, and then press Enter. The appointment is now scheduled for a full hour.

If you need to change an appointment to a different date, you can accomplish this task in the appointment pane as well. Let's move Al Pine's appointment to the day after tomorrow (or the next working day, if that day is a Saturday or Sunday):

1. Point to the border on the left side of the Al Pine appointment and drag it to the correct date on the date navigator.

2. Release the mouse button. Outlook displays the calendar for the new date and enters the appointment in the same time slot.

Editing Recurring Appointments

Editing a recurring appointment works much the same as editing any other type of appointment, except that Outlook gives you the option of changing just one occurrence of the appointment or all of them. Suppose the next client status meeting, which occurs every other Wednesday, will take place in Conference Room A instead of Conference Room B. Follow these steps to change the location of this particular meeting:

Editing one occurrence

1. Click the date of the next client status meeting, and then double-click its box in the appointment pane. Outlook displays this dialog box:

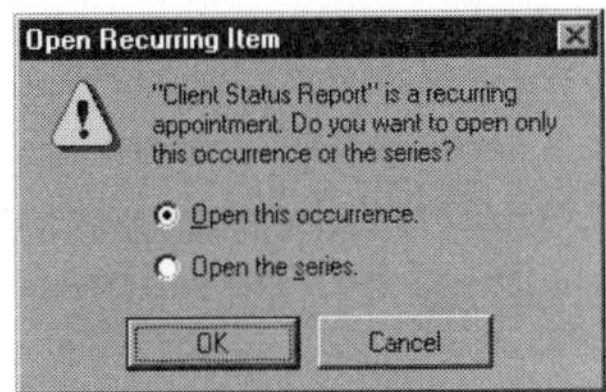

2. You want to change only this occurrence, so click OK to accept the default Open This Occurrence option.
3. When Outlook displays the Recurring Appointment window, change Conference Room B to *Conference Room A* in the Location edit box and click Save And Close.

Canceling Appointments

In addition to editing appointments, you will sometimes need to delete them altogether. Suppose Al Pine has called to cancel his meeting. Follow these steps to delete the appointment from Calendar:

1. Display the Al Pine appointment and click it once to select it.
2. Click the Delete button on the toolbar. Outlook instantly removes the appointment. (If you delete an appointment by mistake, you can choose Undo Delete from the Edit menu to move it back to the appointment pane.)

The procedure for canceling a recurring appointment is much the same as the one for canceling an individual appointment, except that you must decide whether to delete one occurrence of the appointment or all occurrences. You can also convert a recurring appointment to a onetime occurrence. Suppose the senior consultants have decided that after the next client status meeting, client reports will be added to the agenda of a weekly staff meeting instead of being addressed separately. Here's how to make this change:

Canceling recurring appointments

1. Move to the first appointment of the recurring series and then double-click it to display the message that was shown on the previous page.
2. Select the Open The Series option and click OK.

The Recurrence button

3. In the Recurring Appointment window, click the Recurrence button to display the Appointment Recurrence dialog box.
4. Click the Remove Recurrence button.
5. Outlook has changed the Location setting to Conference Room B, so reselect Conference Room A from the Location drop-down list and then click Save And Close in the Appointment window.

By the way, you cannot undo this operation. The only way to restore the recurring appointment is to display its Appointment window, click the Recurrence button, and reenter its information.

Finding Appointments

As your calendar begins to fill up, you may find it increasingly difficult to locate a particular appointment, meeting, or event. If you have a good idea of what you're looking for, you can use the Find button. Follow these steps:

Find

The Find button

1. Click the Find button on the Standard toolbar. (You may have to click More Buttons to display the Find button.) A Find pane opens at the top of the workspace, as shown here:

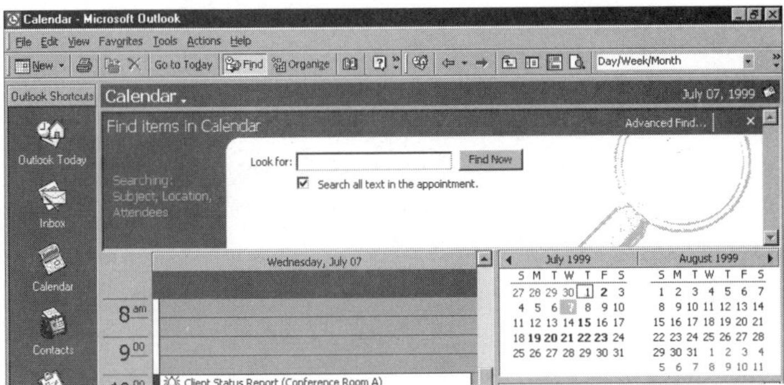

2. In the Look For edit box, type *Dolly Bills*.

3. Click Find Now. Outlook looks in the Subject, Location, and Attendees fields for an appointment that contains the specified words and displays the results in the active appointments table view with a filter applied to the Subject column, as shown here:

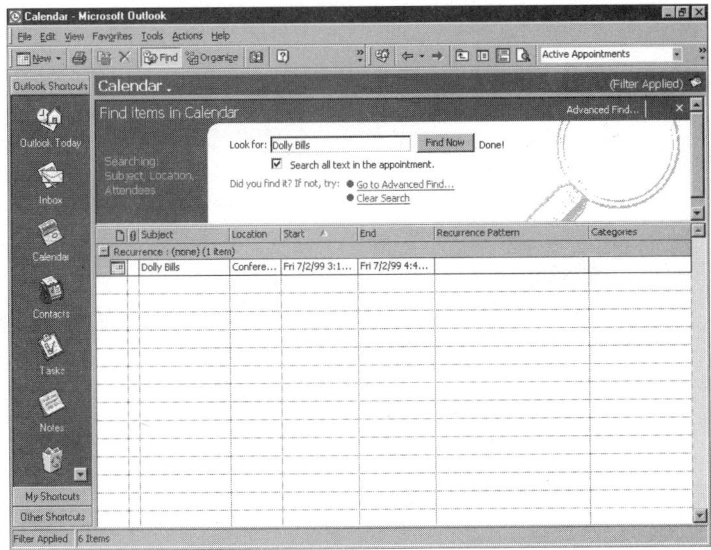

If your search is unsuccessful, you can click Go To Advanced Find (see the adjacent tip) to refine the search, or you can click Clear Search to begin again.

4. Click the Find area's Close button to close the Find pane and return Calendar to its default view.

More complex searches

You can carry out more complex searches by clicking Go To Advanced Find in the Find area. Outlook displays an Advanced Find dialog box very similar to the Filter dialog box shown earlier on page 77. On the Appointments And Meetings tab, you can enter more search criteria. The More Choices and Advanced tabs of the Advanced Find dialog box work the same way as they do in the Filter dialog box. By default, Find searches the currently active Outlook component, but you can change the component by selecting a different option from the Look For drop-down list. Once you finish entering your search criteria, click Find Now to begin the search.

Planning a Meeting

The advent of programs such as Microsoft NetMeeting (see the tip on the facing page) means that you no longer have to be physically present at a meeting to participate. Nevertheless, the face-to-face meeting is still the most common means of communication in the workplace. Whether a meeting is electronic or face-to-face, it needs to be scheduled. If you are working on a network that uses Exchange Server, Calendar can take some of the hassle out of setting up meetings. You can check other people's schedules to determine an appropriate time and place for a meeting and send meeting requests, without the back-and-forth usually involved with such tasks.

Sending Meeting Requests

Suppose you want to set up a meeting for next Wednesday. For this example, you will coordinate schedules and send out a meeting request to just one person, but you will see how easily the procedure could be applied to several people. (If you are not working on a network that uses Exchange Server, read along so that you get an idea of the procedure.) Try this:

Selecting a meeting time

1. With Calendar's contents displayed in the workspace, choose Plan A Meeting from the Actions menu. Outlook then opens the Plan A Meeting dialog box shown below:

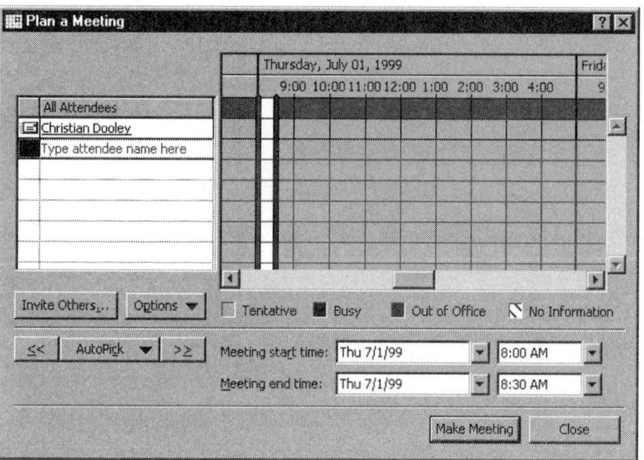

The timeline on the right side of the dialog box displays today's date. If you have any appointments scheduled for today, their time slots are blocked out with colored lines representing the type of appointment (see page 88).

2. You need to schedule a meeting for next Wednesday, so if necessary, change the date in the Meeting Start Time edit box to that date.

Selecting attendees

3. To invite someone to attend the meeting, click the Invite Others button. Outlook displays the dialog box shown below:

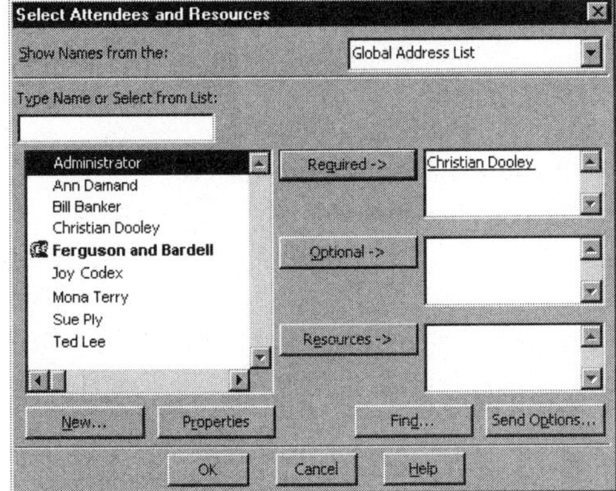

Your name is already entered in the Required box because you are the meeting's organizer. Your name is underlined to indicate that Outlook has information about you, including a valid e-mail address. The names of the people in your network's Global Address List appear in the list box on the left. If necessary, you can change the setting in the Show Names From The box to display the contents of a different address book. (See the tip on page 36 for more information about address books.)

4. Select the name of the person you want to invite from the address book list, click the Required button, and click OK. (If you want to invite someone to the meeting whose presence is desired but not necessary, select his or her name from the address book list, click the Optional button, and click OK.) Notice that Outlook adds a row to the timeline displaying the schedule of the person you want to invite, as you can see at the top of the following page.

Online meetings

To hold a meeting online over the Internet or an intranet, click the This Is An Online Meeting Using check box on the Appointment tab of the Meeting window. The Meeting window then expands so that you can enter a directory server to be used and other information concerning the meeting. By default, Outlook uses NetMeeting for online meetings. You can use NetMeeting to set up audio and video conferences, collaborate on projects, share files, and have onscreen "chat" sessions via the Internet. A full discussion of NetMeeting is beyond the scope of this book. But if you're interested, you might want to check out *Quick Course® in Microsoft Internet Explorer 5* which has an entire chapter devoted to NetMeeting.

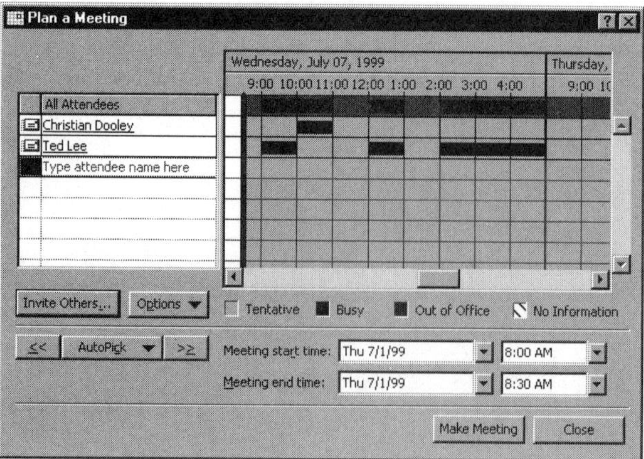

Outlook uses a white bar to highlight the first half-hour time slot available for all attendees.

5. Click AutoPick's >> button to move to the next available time slot. Then either continue clicking until the white bar sits at the time slot you want, or simply click the desired slot. (We selected the 1:30 PM time slot.)

Sending meeting requests

6. To send a meeting request to the person you selected, first click the Make Meeting button. Outlook displays a Meeting window, like this one:

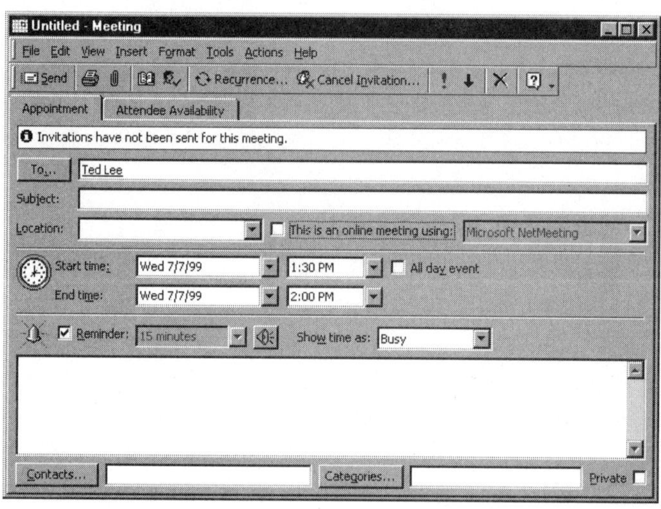

Other ways of requesting meetings

You can also create a meeting request by choosing New Meeting Request from the Actions menu. Instead of displaying the Plan A Meeting dialog box, Outlook displays the Meeting window. Then fill in the information as you would normally. To invite people to the meeting and to check their schedules using this method, use the window's Attendee Availability tab.

7. The selected person's name appears in the To edit box. For demonstration, replace this name with your own.

8. Type *Client Update Meeting* in the Subject edit box and select Conference Room B from the Location drop-down list. Then change the time in the End Time edit box so that the meeting will last one hour.

9. Click an insertion point in the blank note area and type *Hope this time will work for you.*

10. Finally, click the Send button. Outlook sends an e-mail message to the designated address, requesting the meeting at the specified time. Close the dialog box.

Editing Meeting Requests

You may need to add or remove attendees from a meeting request or you may need to change other information, such as the location. Let's try this now:

1. Locate the client update meeting in the appointment pane and double-click its box to display the Meeting window.

2. Change the location to Conference Room A.

3. Click the Attendee Availability tab to display the information shown here:

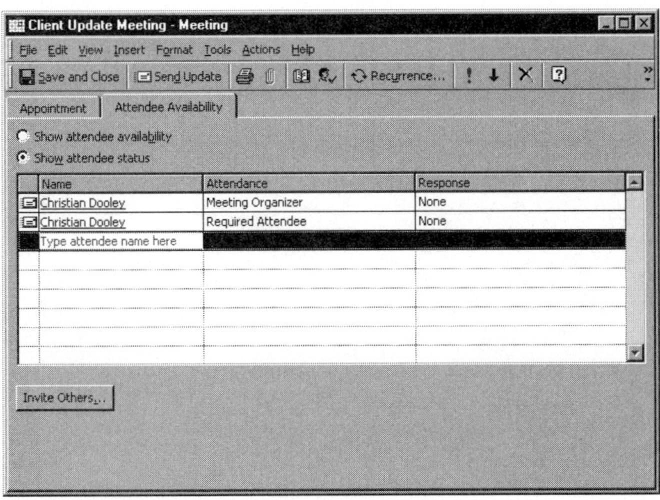

Your name appears as both Meeting Organizer and Required Attendee because you changed the name in step 7 on the facing page. Usually you will see a list of the people whose

Creating recurring meetings

To create a new recurring meeting, first choose New Recurring Meeting from the Actions menu. Fill in the Appointment Recurrence dialog box as usual and click OK. Next fill in the necessary information on the Appointment and Attendee Availability tabs of the Meeting window and click Send. To turn an existing meeting into a recurring one, open the meeting by double-clicking its box in the appointment pane. Then click the Recurrence button to display the Appointment Recurrence dialog box. Fill in the information as usual and then click OK. In the Recurring Meeting window, click the Send Update button so that you can notify all participants of the change.

names you selected in the Select Attendees And Resources dialog box (see page 99). To add or remove attendees, you can click the Invite Others button, add or remove the appropriate people, and then click OK. (Don't make any attendee changes now.)

Adding or removing meeting attendees

Send Update

The Send Update button

4. To notify the attendees of the location change, click the Send Update button on the toolbar. Outlook sends a new e-mail message to the meeting attendees (in this case, just you) and closes the Meeting window.

Responding to Meeting Requests

Now that you know how to request a meeting, you need to see what to do if you receive a meeting request. Follow these steps to respond to the request you just sent yourself:

1. Display the contents of the Inbox in the workspace and, if necessary, click the Send/Receive button to check for new messages.
2. After you receive the messages regarding the meeting, open the first meeting request you sent. It displays a message stating the request is out-of-date. (Outlook adds this notification because the meeting request has been updated.)
3. Close the window and then open the second message, which looks like this:

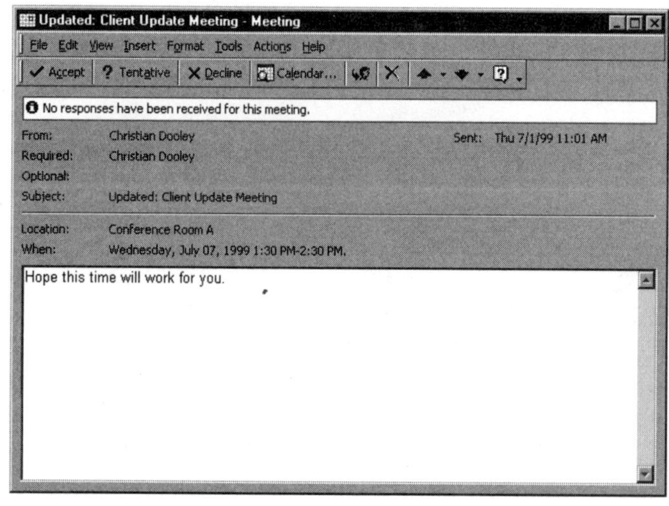

Canceling meetings

If you need to cancel a meeting, first open it in its Meeting window. Then choose Cancel Meeting from the window's Actions menu. Outlook displays a message that gives you the option of deleting the meeting and sending cancellation notices to all attendees or deleting the meeting without sending the cancellation notice. Select the option you want and then click OK. If you are sending cancellation notices, be sure to click the Send button in the Meeting window before closing it. If you receive a meeting cancellation notice, you can click the Remove From Calendar button to delete the meeting from your calendar.

At the top of the window, Outlook displays a message that no responses have been received for the meeting. If a conflict in your schedule means the requested meeting time won't work for you, Outlook also informs you of the conflict. Toolbar buttons provide three options for responding to the meeting request. You can accept, tentatively accept, or decline.

4. Choose Calendar from the window's View menu to check whether the meeting fits with your schedule. Then click the message window's button on the Windows taskbar to redisplay the meeting message.
5. Click the appropriate response button to send your reply to the meeting organizer. In this case, because you are the meeting organizer, Outlook displays a message saying no response is needed. Click OK to close the message box.
6. Close the Meeting window. (You might want to delete the two meeting requests from your Inbox before moving on. You can also cancel the meeting by following the instructions in the tip on the facing page.)

Customizing Calendar

The Calendar component of Outlook can be tailored using the customization features we discussed in earlier chapters. However, we also want to show you different ways you can view schedules in Calendar and additional ways of customizing Calendar to make it easier to use.

The first three Calendar views are grouped in one category called *day/week/month*. By default, Calendar displays your schedules in day view, meaning it displays your schedule for one day only, with the times at half-hour intervals along the left side of the appointment pane. Let's look at some ways you can customize day view:

1. To change the time interval, right-click any time to display a shortcut menu. Notice that you can choose an interval from 5 to 60 minutes from the bottom section of the menu.
2. Choose 15 Minutes from the shortcut menu. The appointment pane now looks like the one shown on the next page.

More Calendar options

You can set options that relate to meetings by choosing Options from the Tools menu and clicking Calendar Options on the Preferences tab to display the Calendar Options dialog box. If you click the Resource Scheduling button, you can set options to automatically accept or decline certain types of meeting requests. If you click the Free/Busy Options button, you can enter how many months of your schedule are posted on the network server, as well as how often your schedule gets updated on the server.

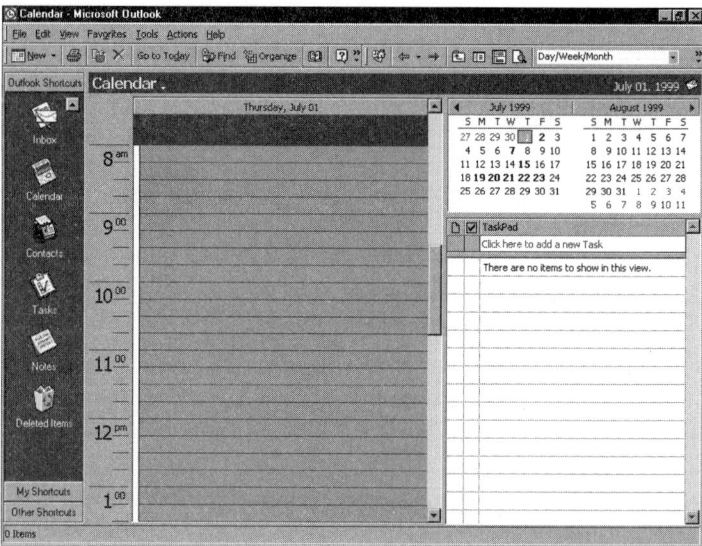

Outlook keeps track of time-zone information based on specifications made when Windows was installed on your computer. If necessary, you can change or add a time zone directly in Outlook. Let's add another time zone to the appointment pane so that you can keep track of things in the London office of Ferguson and Bardell:

Adding a time zone

1. Choose Options from the Tools menu, and on the Preferences tab, click the Calendar Options button.
2. Click the Time Zone button in the Calendar Options section. Outlook displays this dialog box:

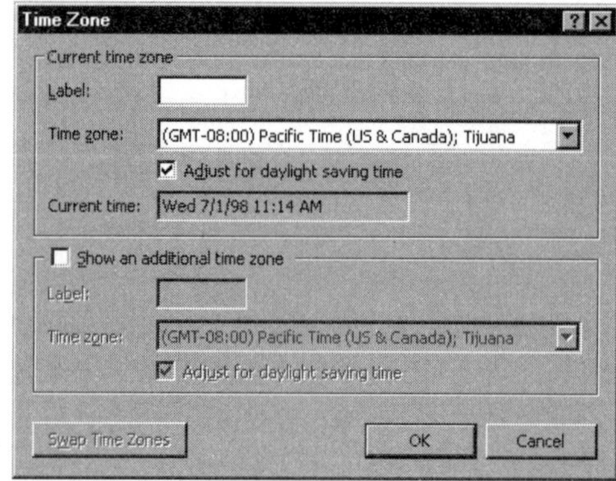

3. In the Label edit box of the Current Time Zone section, type *Seattle*.

4. Next click the Show An Additional Time Zone check box, type *London* in the Label edit box, select the (GMT) Greenwich Mean Time option from about the middle of the Time Zone drop-down list, and click OK three times. The appointment pane now looks like this:

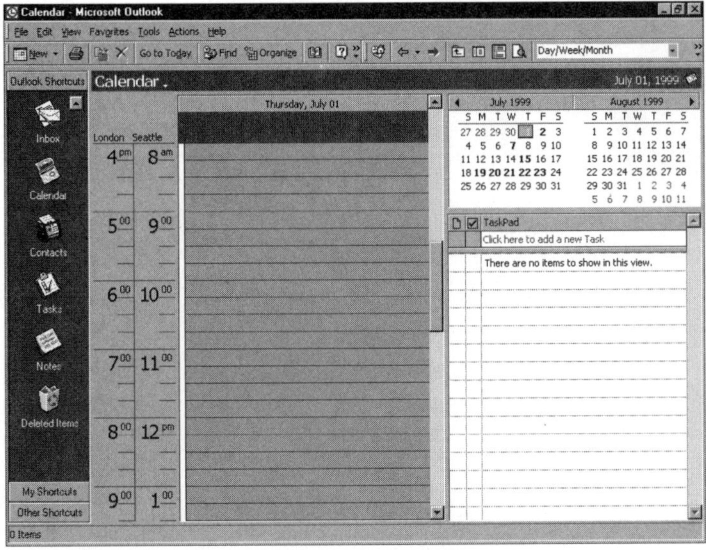

Removing a time zone

5. To remove the London time zone, right-click the time-slot area, choose Change Time Zone from the shortcut menu, and deselect the Show An Additional Time Zone check box. Then delete the Seattle label and click OK.

To display more than one day in the appointment pane, you can switch to week view (seven days) or work week view (five days). Or, you can survey the entire month in month view. Let's take a look at these views now:

1. If necessary, drag the Advanced toolbar's move handle to the right until the Day, Work Week, Week, and Month buttons all appear on the Standard toolbar.

The Week button

2. Click the Week button to change Calendar's display to look like the one shown at the top of the next page.

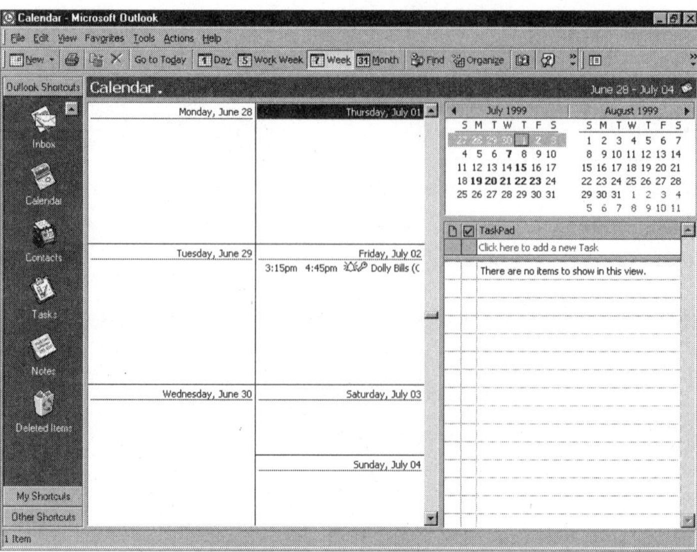

The date navigator and TaskPad remain the same, but the appointment pane changes to display the appointments for the current week. All the information pertaining to each appointment is included.

The Month button

3. Click the Month button to change Calendar's display to look like this:

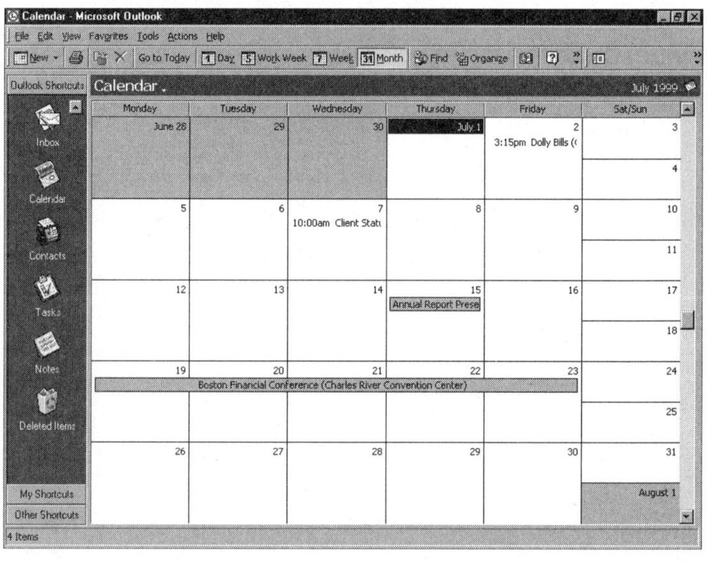

Printing schedules

To print a calendar, choose Print from the File menu or click the Print button on the toolbar. Then select a print style and any other options you want in the Print dialog box, and click OK. If you're not sure what style you want, select one of the style options and click the Preview button. You can also specify the dates you want to print in the Print Range section of the Print dialog box.

The date navigator and TaskPad have disappeared. If all the appointments for a particular day won't fit in the appointment pane, Outlook displays a yellow arrow button indicating that information is hidden. Clicking this button displays that day's calendar in day view.

The Day button

4. Click the Day button to return to the default day view with the selected date displayed.

   Calendar's remaining views are accessible through the Current View box on the Advanced toolbar. Each view (except the by category view) sorts appointments by recurrence group first and then in chronological order. The by category view sorts appointments by their assigned categories. As you experiment with the different views, remember that you can customize them by grouping items or by defining new views.

   That wraps up this chapter on the Calendar component of Outlook. Now that you know the in's and out's of using this feature, you'll have no more excuses for forgetting appointments or being late to meetings!

5 Keeping a To-Do List

By using Outlook's Tasks component, you can keep track of tasks and projects in an electronic to-do list. In this chapter, we show how to manage and prioritize onetime and recurring tasks, as well as how to delegate them to other people.

You can track both business and personal tasks in Outlook's to-do list. And whether you work alone or need to coordinate tasks with others, Outlook can help you monitor your progress and keep you on track.

Tasks performed and concepts covered:

Enter tasks that need to be performed repeatedly at regular intervals

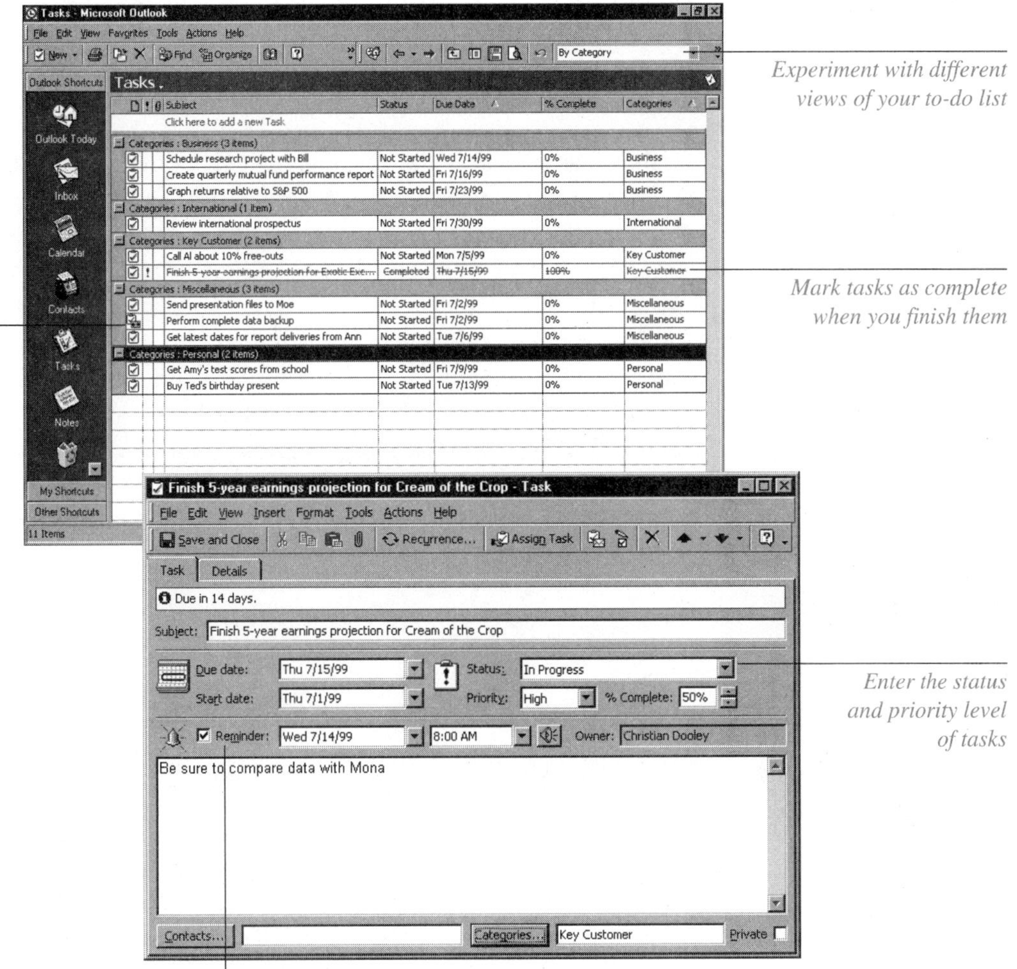

Experiment with different views of your to-do list

Mark tasks as complete when you finish them

Enter the status and priority level of tasks

Set due dates and reminder times for tasks

As your schedule becomes increasingly busy, you may have trouble juggling the many tasks you need to perform during the day. To make matters more complicated, you may be trying to get personal tasks done as well as business tasks. In the past, you may have kept track of the things you needed to do either in your head or on pieces of paper (with varying degrees of legibility). Now you can use Outlook's Tasks component to create efficient, readable, and organized to-do lists.

Using Tasks, not only can you manage and prioritize your work, but if necessary, you can also schedule time in your calendar for specific tasks. If you are working on a network that uses Exchange Server, other people in your company can then check your schedule and see that you are unavailable for meetings and appointments during the time you plan to work on a task. (For more information, see "Planning a Meeting" on page 98.) In this chapter, we discuss how to add tasks to your to-do list and how to deal with the tasks at various stages. We also show you ways to organize tasks to make the best use of this Outlook component, and how to electronically delegate tasks to coworkers.

Adding Tasks

You don't have to do anything to create a to-do list because Outlook has already taken care of that task for you. But before you can do anything with the list, you need to add some tasks to it. When Calendar is displayed in the Outlook workspace, you can add tasks by clicking the new-task area at the top of the TaskPad. In this chapter, however, you'll work directly with the Tasks component. You'll start by adding a simple task to get familiar with the process. Then to learn about more complex task options, you'll add a task with a deadline and one designated as a high priority. Follow these steps:

The Tasks icon

1. With Outlook open on your screen, click the Tasks icon on the Outlook bar to open the empty to-do list shown at the top of the facing page.

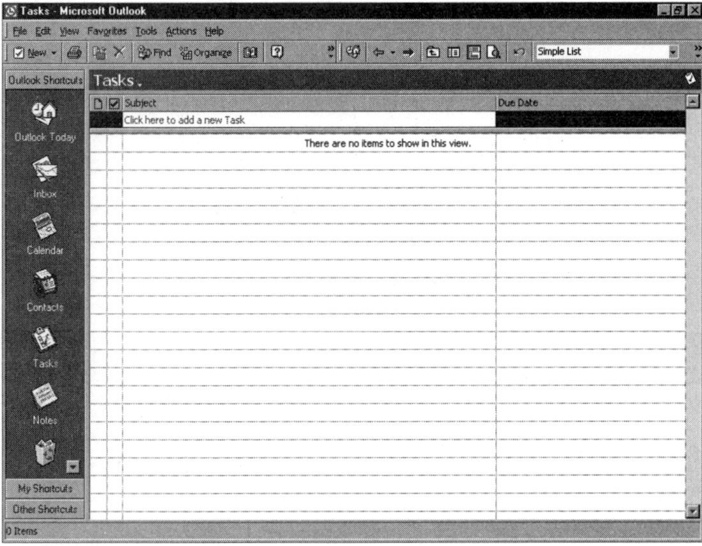

Your to-do list may list a sample task, but if it looks different from ours otherwise, change the setting in the Current View box to Simple List. (We discuss other views on page 118.) You see four columns of information:

- **The Icon column.** The icon indicates the type of item. (In most cases, the item will be a regular task.)
- **The Complete column.** If you designate the task as complete, this column displays a check mark in a box.
- **The Subject column.** This column displays the description entered for the task, such as *Send get-well card to Mona.*
- **The Due Date column.** If you set no due date, this column contains the word *None*.

2. Click *Click Here To Add A New Task* in the Subject column, and type *Pick up dry cleaning*.
3. Click None in the Due Date column to display an arrow, and then click the arrow to display a drop-down calendar.
4. Select tomorrow's date from the calendar.

Now suppose you want to add an important task that must be completed by tomorrow afternoon. By default, tasks have no

Other ways to add tasks

If you want to add a task while working in another Outlook component, you can click the arrow to the right of the New button and then select Task; press Ctrl+Shift+K; or choose New and then Task from the File menu. If you are working in Word, Excel, or PowerPoint, you can create a new task that is automatically linked to your open document. (You must save the document for the link to take effect.) First display the Reviewing toolbar by right-clicking an open toolbar and choosing Reviewing from the shortcut menu. Then click the Create Microsoft Outlook Task button to display a Task window with a shortcut to the file in the message area of the window.

due date, have not yet started, and have normal priority. Follow the steps below to enter start and due dates and assign a priority level:

The New Task button

1. Click the New Task button to display this window:

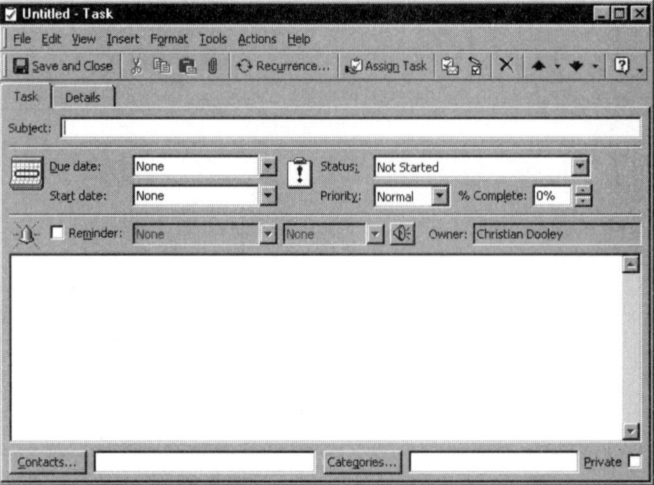

2. Type *Create quarterly mutual fund performance report* in the Subject edit box. Then click the arrow to the right of the Due Date edit box, and when the calendar appears, click tomorrow's date.

Setting a priority level

3. Change the Priority setting to High, and then click Save And Close. As you can see here, your two tasks are now listed in the workspace:

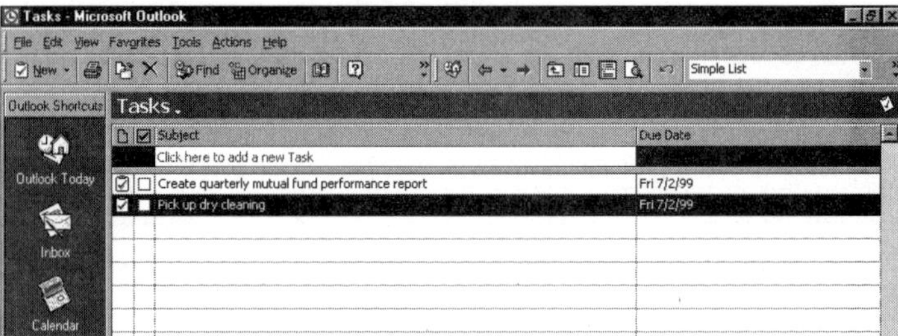

Now let's add one more task, using a few more of the options available in the Task window:

1. Click the New Task button to open a Task window, and type *Finish 5-year earnings projection for Cream of the Crop* in the Subject edit box.
2. Click the arrow to the right of the Due Date edit box, and in the drop-down calendar, select the date two weeks from today. Then change the Start Date setting to today's date.
3. Click the arrow to the right of the Status edit box to show a list of options. You have already started this project, so select In Progress.

Changing a task's status

4. Next change the Priority setting to High.
5. This project is about half-finished, so click the up arrow to the right of the % Complete edit box twice to display 50%.

Indicating progress

6. Now change the reminder date and time to the day before the project is due at 8:00 AM.

Setting a reminder

7. Click an insertion point in the message box at the bottom of the dialog box and type *Be sure to compare data with Mona.*
8. Finally, click the Categories button, click the Key Customer check box, and click OK. The Task window looks like this:

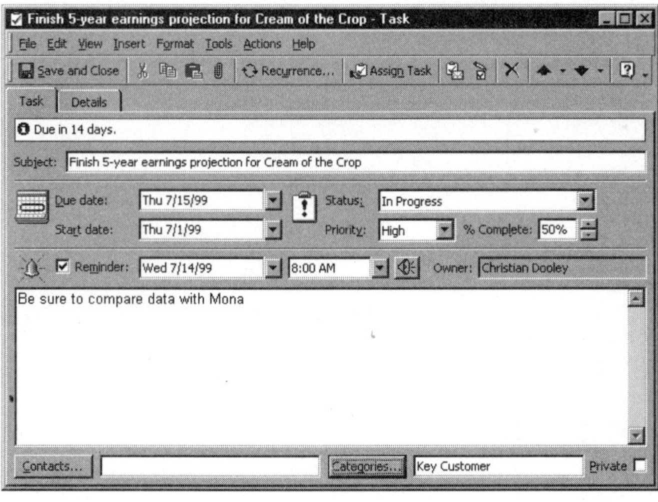

9. Click Save And Close to add the task to your to-do list.

Creating tasks from messages and appointments

If you receive an e-mail message that contains a task you need to add to your to-do list, or if you need to create a task based on an appointment entered in the Calendar, you can use AutoCreate to streamline the process. To convert an e-mail message into a task, select its header in the Inbox and drag it to the Tasks icon. Outlook then opens the Task window with the message text displayed in the bottom area. Fill in the remaining information (such as priority and due date) and then click Save And Close. To create a task based on an appointment, drag the appointment from the appointment pane to the Tasks icon. Complete the new task information and save it as usual.

Adding Recurring Tasks

Now suppose that on every other Friday, you have to perform a complete backup of the files you have created on your computer. To add a recurring task to your to-do list, you first create the task, then designate it as recurring. Follow these steps:

1. Click the New Task button on the toolbar and type *Perform complete data backup* in the Subject edit box.
2. Click the Recurrence button to display a dialog box similar to the one shown on page 90.
3. Check that Weekly is selected in the Recurrence Pattern section, and change the Recur Every option to 2 weeks. Select the Friday check box (the check boxes for all other days should be deselected), and change the date in the Start box to this coming Friday. The dialog box now looks like this:

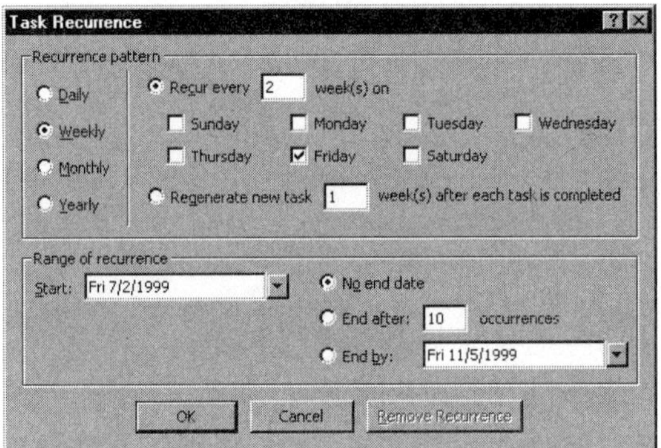

4. Click OK to close the Task Recurrence dialog box.
5. Back in the Task window, change the Reminder time to 1:00 PM and then click Save And Close. (In the to-do list, notice that Outlook displays a recurring icon for the data backup task in the Icon column.)

Setting reminder times

By default, task reminder times are set for 8:00 AM. However, if you would prefer to be reminded at a different time of day, you can change the default setting. Choose Options from the Tools menu, and in the Tasks section of the Preferences tab, type a new time in the Reminder Time edit box; or click the arrow to the right of the box to select a time from the drop-down list. Then click OK.

Editing Tasks

After creating a task, you may sometimes notice a typographical error that needs to be fixed or an item of information, such as a due date, that needs to be changed. You can make some changes directly in the to-do list, or you can reopen the Task window. Let's try both methods:

1. Click the earnings projection task and then select *Cream of the Crop*.
2. Replace the highlighted text with *Exotic Excursions* and then press Enter.

Now suppose your supervisor has informed you that, because of some database problems, the quarterly mutual fund performance report cannot be completed for another two weeks. Let's change its due date and priority level:

1. Double-click the performance report task to display its Task window.
2. Change the due date to two weeks from tomorrow and then reset the Priority to Normal.
3. Click Save And Close to update the task.

Designating Tasks as Complete

Adding tasks to the to-do list is only the first step if you want to manage your time effectively. You must also keep the status of your tasks up-to-date. Outlook provides several methods for showing that a task is complete.

Suppose you have picked up the dry cleaning and finished the Exotic Excursions 5-year earnings projection. Let's try a couple of different methods to show that these tasks are complete:

1. Click the check box in the Complete column of the dry cleaning task to designate the task as finished, as shown here:

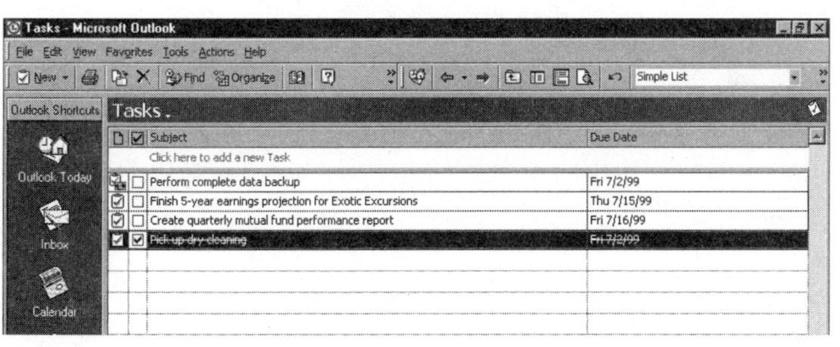

Copying tasks

Occasionally, you may want to create a new task that is similar to an existing one. You can speed up the process by copying the existing task. First select the task you want to copy. Then hold down the Ctrl key and the left mouse button and drag the task to the Tasks icon on the Outlook bar. Release the mouse button and then the Ctrl key. (You can also use the Copy and Paste commands on the Edit menu to copy a task.) Then open the copy's Task window and make any necessary changes.

When you mark a task as complete, Outlook displays a check mark in the check box, changes the font's color to gray, and crosses out the task text. It does not delete the task from the list. This way, you can view the list and double-check that you did in fact complete the task. (If Outlook simply erased the task, you might not remember whether you ever added it to the list in the first place.)

The Mark Complete button

2. Next double-click the earnings projection task to display its Task window and then click the Mark Complete button on the window's toolbar. Outlook closes the window and changes the display of the task in the to-do list to show that it is complete. (You can also change the Status edit box to Completed and then click Save And Close.)

If you want, you can use the % Complete field to record the status of the task, and you can change it to 100% to show that the task is finished. To update this field, you can display the Task window or make changes directly in the % Complete field shown in detailed list view. (We discuss this view on page 118.)

The Details tab

When creating or editing a task, you can use the Details tab of the Task window to keep track of additional information about the task. Outlook automatically fills in the Date Completed field with the date on which you mark the task as complete. In the Total Work field, you can enter the total number of hours you think the task will take to complete, and in the Actual Work field, you can enter the real number of hours it took. You use the remaining four fields to track mileage, billing information, and contacts or companies associated with the task. If you are working on a network that uses Exchange Server and you assign this task to a co-worker (see page 120), the Update List section lists all people whose task lists must be updated if a change is made to a task.

Deleting Completed Tasks

If you complete a task and no longer want to keep it on your to-do list, you can delete it. (Sometimes you may even want to delete an unfinished task.) Here's how to remove a task from the to-do list:

1. Click the dry cleaning task to select it.
2. Now click the Delete button on the toolbar to remove the task from the list.
3. Delete any other tasks you don't need on your list, being sure to leave the three tasks you added in this chapter.

Like the deleted items of other components, Outlook moves deleted tasks to the Deleted Items folder. They will remain there until you either erase them from the folder or empty the folder completely.

Organizing Tasks

Now that you know how to add, edit, and delete tasks, we'll discuss some ways in which to categorize and organize them for maximum efficiency. As with other Outlook components, you can change the view of the to-do list. But before you take a look at the different views available for the Tasks component, we'll show you a quick way to reorganize the list. Follow these steps:

1. First add about eight more tasks to your to-do list using any of the methods we've discussed, so that you have a slightly longer list to work with. The tasks will be listed in the order in which you entered them, with the most recent entry at the top of the list.

2. You might find it more useful to list the tasks in Due Date order. Click the Due Date column header once to quickly reorganize the list chronologically by due date. Notice that Outlook has reorganized the list in descending order, symbolized by the down arrow in the column header.

3. To switch to ascending order, simply click the column header again. The list now looks like this:

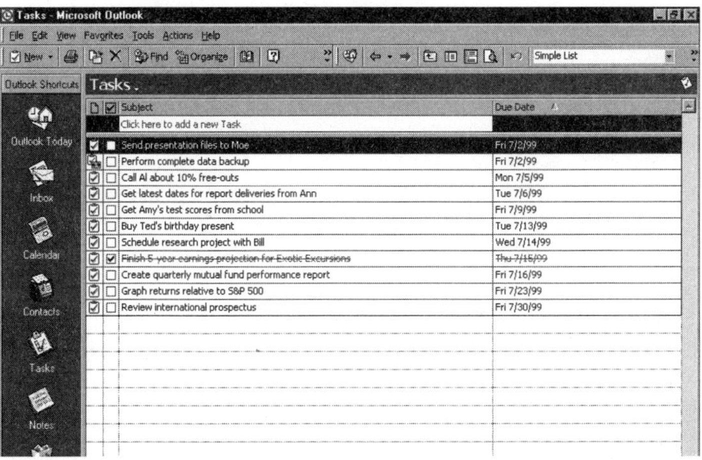

Let's take a look at other Tasks views. Follow the steps on the next page.

Changing task text color schemes

By default, Outlook changes a completed task's text to gray and marks past due tasks in red. If you want to change the color scheme, choose Options from the Tools menu, and on the Preferences tab, click the Task Options button. In the dialog box that appears, click the arrow to the right of the Overdue Tasks or Completed Tasks edit box and select a new color from the drop-down list. Once you decide on a new color scheme, click OK twice to implement your changes.

Switching views

1. Click the arrow to the right of the Current View box to drop-down a list of ten view options.

2. Select Detailed List to display the to-do list like this:

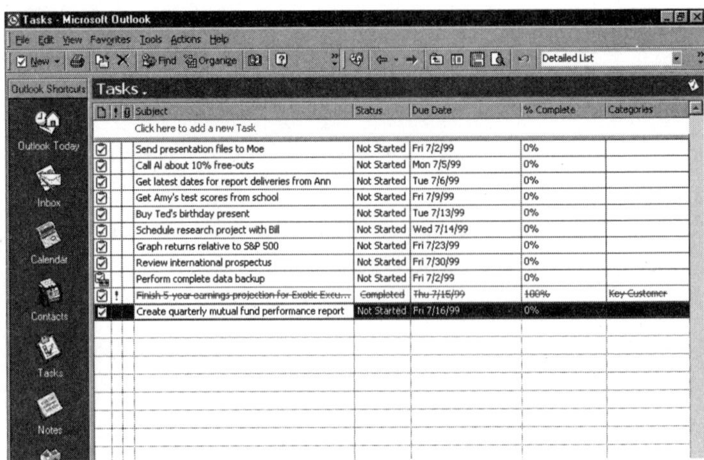

This view displays the Icon, Priority, Attachment, Subject, Status, Due Date, % Complete, and Categories fields. Notice that the high priority task is flagged with an exclamation mark in the Priority column.

Before you look at the next view, you need to assign all the tasks to categories. Being able to categorize tasks is particularly useful if you work concurrently on different projects, or if you like to keep track of personal as well as business tasks. Let's categorize the tasks now:

Assigning tasks to categories

1. Select the first task, right-click any field except the active one, and choose Categories from the shortcut menu to display the Categories dialog box shown earlier on page 15.

2. Select the appropriate category from the list and click OK. (You can assign the same task to more than one category.)

3. Repeat this procedure for the remaining tasks. When you finish, your to-do list looks something like the one at the top of the facing page.

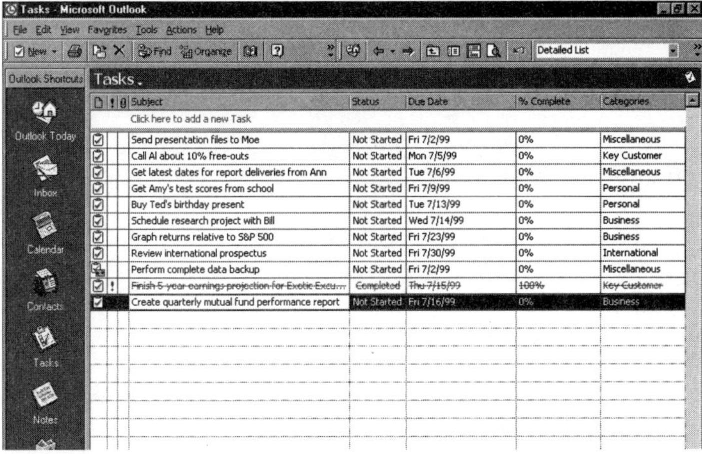

Now you're ready to use the by category view to look at the to-do list. Follow these steps:

1. Change the Current View setting to By Category.
2. Click the plus sign next to each category to display its contents like this:

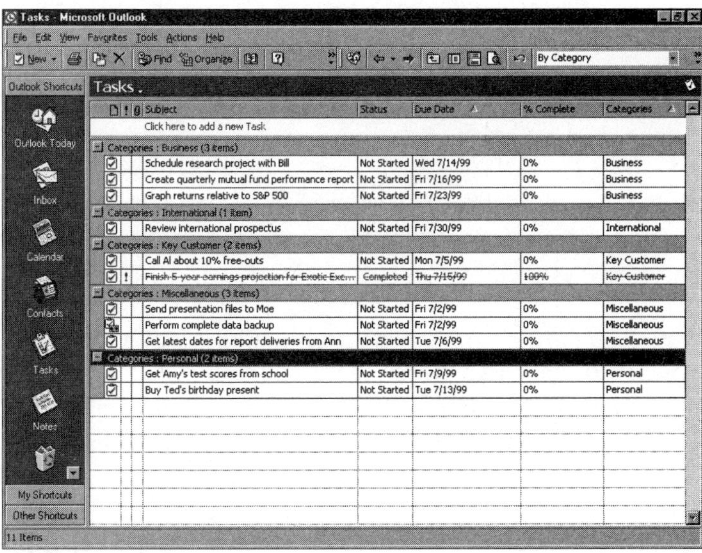

This view displays the same fields as the detailed list view, but rearranges the tasks by category. (By default, the categories are sorted alphabetically in ascending order, and within each category, the tasks are sorted by due date in ascending order.) If you have assigned a task to more than one category, it appears in both places.

3. Experiment with some of the other tasks views (see the adjacent tip), and then return to the simple list view.

Remember, you can customize any of these views or create completely new ones (see page 21).

Delegating Tasks

Before we wrap up this discussion of the Tasks component, we want to quickly discuss one more useful feature. If you are using Outlook on a stand-alone computer, you can skip this section because it pertains only to those of you working with Outlook on a network that uses Exchange Server.

If you are a manager or supervisor, part of your job is to delegate tasks to ensure that your company's business is carried out efficiently and economically. And you will probably need to keep tabs on the status of the tasks you delegate. Outlook's Tasks component can help you with these chores. Although we don't recommend eliminating face-to-face communication with your colleagues, we do suggest you experiment with this feature to see if it can help you manage projects better. Let's try it out now:

1. With the Tasks component active, choose New Task Request from the Actions menu to display a window similar to the standard Task window.

2. In the To edit box, type the e-mail address of the person to whom you want to delegate the task. (You can also click the To button to display the Select Task Recipient dialog box, which works like the Select Names dialog box shown on page 67.)

3. In the Subject edit box, type *Finish reviewing Cream of the Crop annual report.*

Other tasks views

You may want to experiment with other tasks views to help you organize your day. The active tasks view displays the same fields as the detailed list view for the tasks that have not been designated as complete. The next seven days view displays only the tasks with due dates within the next week. The overdue tasks view displays tasks that have slipped through the cracks. The assignment view displays the tasks you have given to others but that you track with an updated copy. The by person responsible view groups assigned tasks by the people who now own them. The completed tasks view lets you view what you have accomplished. Finally, the task timeline view shows the start date and due date of a task (if that information was entered in the Task window) and when both dates are known, a gray bar indicates the interval between them on a timeline. You can change the timeline by clicking the Day, Week, or Month buttons on the toolbar.

4. Click the arrow to the right of the Due Date edit box and assign a date two weeks from today.

5. Change the Status setting to In Progress and then change the Priority setting to High. Next assign the task to the Key Customer category. The task now looks something like the one shown below:

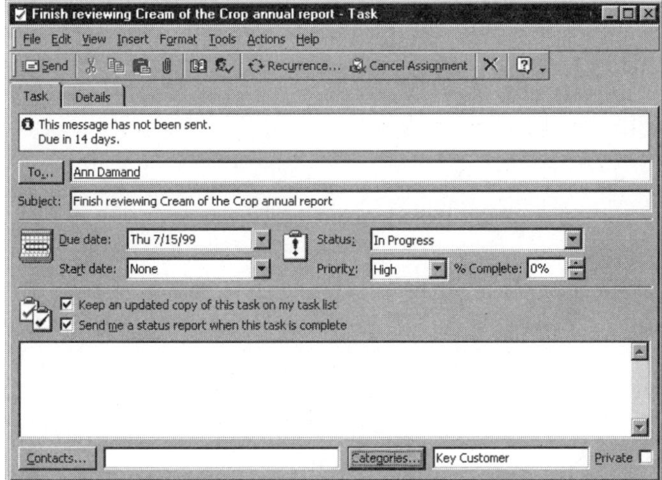

Notice the two check boxes above the message area of the window. If the Keep An Updated Copy check box is selected, Tasks tracks the progress of the task on a copy of it in your to-do list even if you assign the task to someone else and no longer "own" it. If the Send Me A Status Report check box is selected, the task recipient (the new "owner") can easily keep you posted on the task's status by clicking the Send Status Report button in the Task window. This creates a status report addressed to you (the original owner). Note that if these check boxes are not selected, then the task is removed from your to-do list once the person you have delegated it to accepts it.

6. To send the task, you would click the Send button. You won't actually send this task, so go ahead and click the Close button and then click No when Outlook asks if you want to save your changes.

Owning tasks

Every time you create a new task, Outlook automatically designates you as the "owner" of the task unless you specify otherwise by assigning the task to someone else. If someone else accepts the task, he or she becomes the new owner even though you were the one who initially created the task. Bear in mind that when you assign a task to several people, Outlook designates the first person listed in the To edit box as the owner of the task.

When you send a task assignment, the task shows up in your to-do list with a hand attached to the task's icon. If the recipient accepts or declines the task, notification shows up in your Inbox. Double-clicking the notification displays the Task window, which notes whether the task has been accepted. If the task has been declined, you can reassign the task. First you must return the open task to your own to-do list by clicking the Return To Task List button. Then you can reassign the task by clicking the Assign Task button and completing the boxes in the Task window as usual.

Dealing with a Task Request

If you are working on a network that uses Exchange Server and someone else delegates a task to you, you receive the task request in your Inbox, just like a meeting request or an e-mail message. (The task is also added to your to-do list in bold type, indicating that you have yet to respond to it.) You can open the message and respond to it using the Accept, Decline, or Assign Task buttons on the window's toolbar. When you accept or decline a task, Outlook displays a dialog box giving you the option of either editing the response or sending the response immediately.

If you accept the task, it remains in your to-do list, and you become its owner, meaning you can make changes to its status, deadline, and so on. If you decline a task, the task is returned to the original owner, who can then reassign it. If you assign the task to someone else, either in the original request message or after accepting it, you follow the procedure for assigning an existing task described in the tip below.

Assigning existing tasks

If you want to assign an existing task to someone else, open its Task window and click the Assign Task button on the toolbar. The standard Task window is then converted into a Task Request window, where you fill in the information as usual and then click Send.

Reassigning tasks

Suppose you have assigned a task but now want to give it to a different colleague. If you selected the Keep An Updated Copy check box in the original Task Request window, you can open the updated copy of the task in your own to-do list. Next click the Details tab and click the Create Unassigned Copy button. (See the tip on page 116 for more information about the Details tab.) Click OK in the message box that appears. You can then edit the copy of the original task request and send it to the new recipient(s). (Obviously, you will need to notify the person to whom you originally designated the task of the change.)

That ends our discussion of Outlook's Tasks component. The more diligent you are about using and updating your to-do list, the more Outlook can help you keep your life on track. Also remember that the usefulness of Outlook's Tasks component is augmented by the fact that a small version of the to-do list is displayed in the Calendar, which makes it easy to schedule time slots for specific tasks so that nothing slips through the cracks.

6

Checking Ahead and Looking Back

You fire up Outlook Today to see an overview of all the things you need to do today. Then you explore the Journal component, adding specific Outlook activities and documents to its log. Finally, you learn how to archive old Outlook items.

With Journal, you can keep track of how you've spent your time. You can then use this information as a basis for assessing project costs, consultant fees, or volunteer hours for your organization or community group.

Tasks performed and concepts covered:

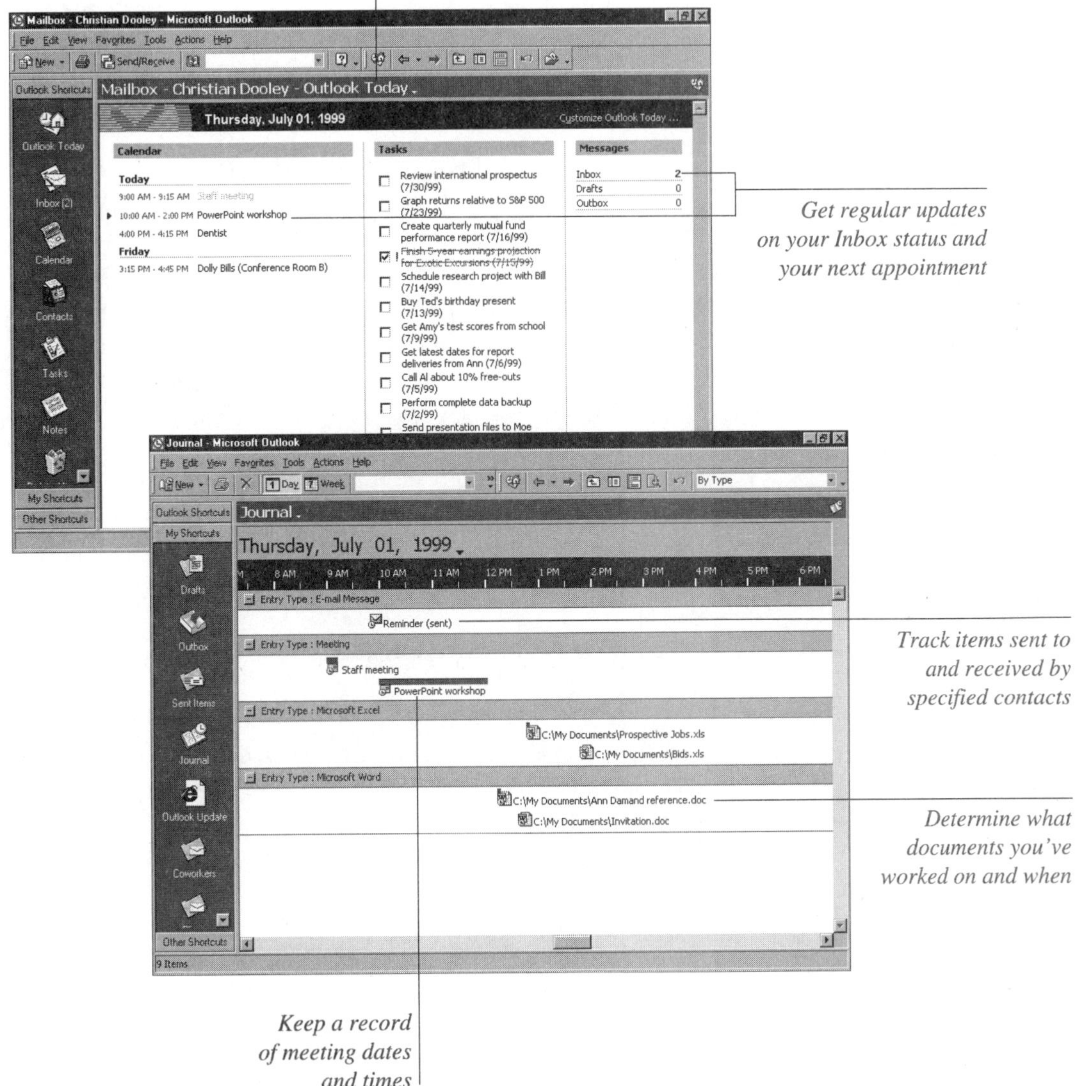

So far, we have discussed the components of Outlook that you will probably use most frequently. As you'll see in a moment, displaying Outlook Today in the workspace allows you to check the contents of these components simultaneously and gives you an overview of what you need to do today. You can also use the Journal component to get an overview of what you've already done. In this chapter, you'll take a brief look at Outlook's summary of what today has in store for you, and then you'll focus on how to look back at your past efforts.

Using Outlook Today

There's nothing complicated about Outlook Today. It simply gathers information from Calendar, Tasks, and the Inbox and summarizes them on one convenient screen. Now that you have entries in these three components, let's display Outlook Today in the workspace and then work with it a bit:

The Outlook Today icon

1. Click the Outlook Today icon on the Outlook bar to display an overview of the things you need to do, as shown below. (We have added some appointments to Calendar and sent ourselves a couple of messages for purposes of demonstration.)

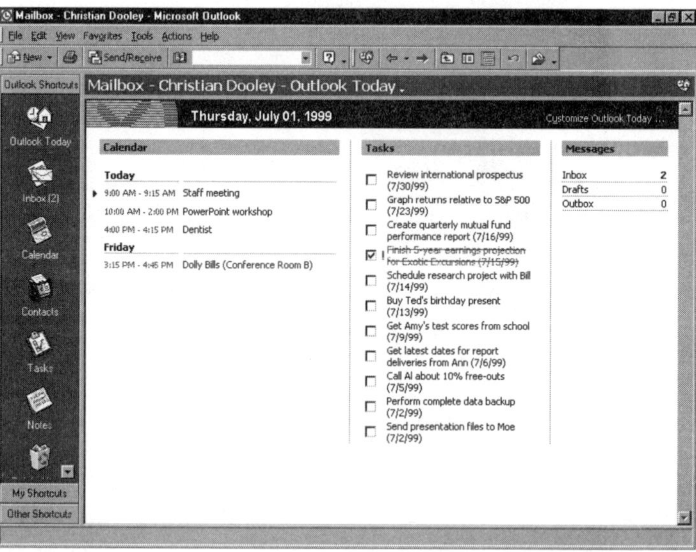

Notice that your next appointment is flagged with an arrow. The subjects of any appointments that have already occurred appear in gray type.

Marking tasks as complete in Outlook Today

2. Suppose you have finished the graphing task. Click its check box in the Tasks section. Outlook puts a check mark in the check box and strikes through the task text, like this:

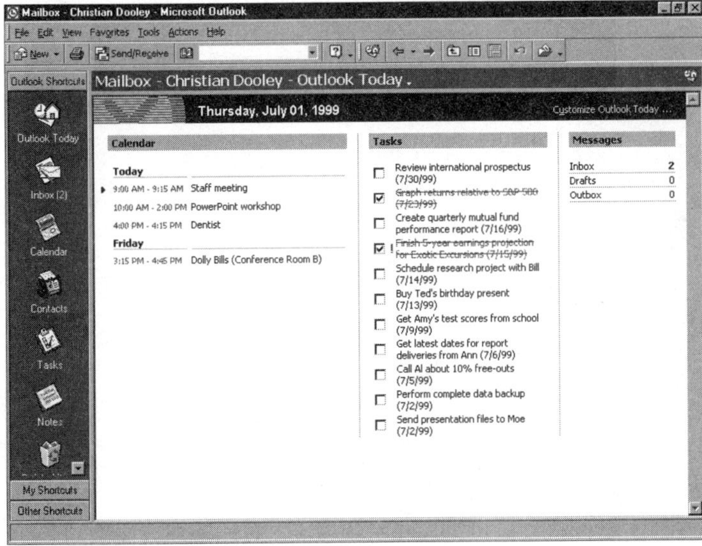

Jumping to other components

3. Click the Tasks section heading to display the contents of Tasks in the workspace. Notice that the graphing task is marked as completed there, too. (You can click any section heading to jump directly to the corresponding component.)

4. Click the Outlook Today icon to return to the workload summary.

Making Outlook Today the Starting Component

By default, the Inbox is the Outlook component displayed in the workspace when you start the program. After you enter information in Calendar and Tasks and start receiving e-mail messages, you will probably want to see a more complete picture when you start Outlook. Follow the steps on the next page to change the default starting component.

Finding contacts

When Outlook Today is displayed in the workspace, you can quickly locate contact information by clicking the Find A Contact box on the Standard toolbar. (This button is also available from other components.) Type the name of the contact in the box and then press Enter to display the contact's address card without having to switch to the Contact's component.

Customizing Outlook Today

1. In the top right corner of the workspace, click Customize Outlook Today. The workspace changes to display this list of the ways you can customize the Outlook Today screen:

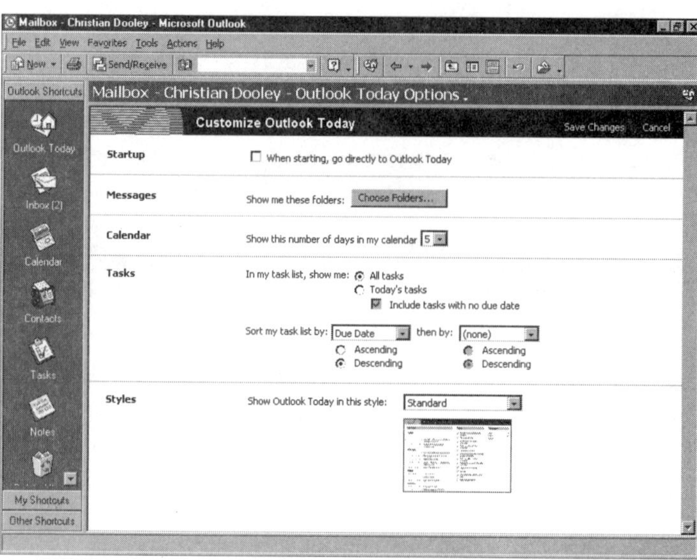

2. In the Startup section, click the When Starting, Go Directly To Outlook Today check box.

3. Click Save Changes to return to Outlook Today.

Now whenever you start Outlook, the program will gather information about your workload and display it for you.

Other Outlook Today options

In the Customize Outlook Today workspace, you can click the Choose Folders button in the Messages section and then select which folders you want to appear in that section of Outlook Today. In the Calendar section, you can designate how many days of your schedule you want displayed by clicking the arrow to the right of the Show This Number edit box and then selecting a number from the drop-down list. In the Tasks section, you can tell Outlook whether to show all tasks or just the tasks for today, whether to list tasks that have no deadline, and how to sort the tasks. In the Style section, you can select from a drop-down list of predefined styles that control how Outlook Today displays its information.

Using Journal

As you work with Outlook, the Journal component can be active behind the scenes, logging the tasks you perform on the computer, including Outlook activities and the documents you create with Microsoft Office applications. You can record your own journal entries and track your interactions with designated contacts. Then if you need to know how many hours you worked on a report in Word, or you want to check when you last e-mailed a client, you can easily track down this information. Journal can also help you keep Outlook efficient by archiving old information.

First let's take a look at Journal, and then we'll show you what you can do with it. Follow these steps:

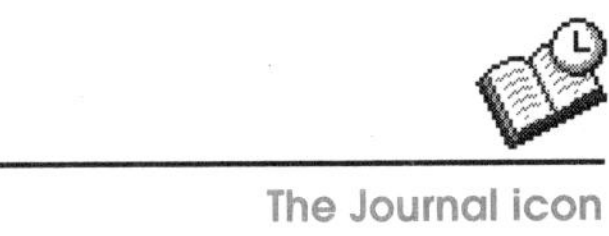

The Journal icon

1. Open the My Shortcuts group and click the Journal icon. You see this dialog box:

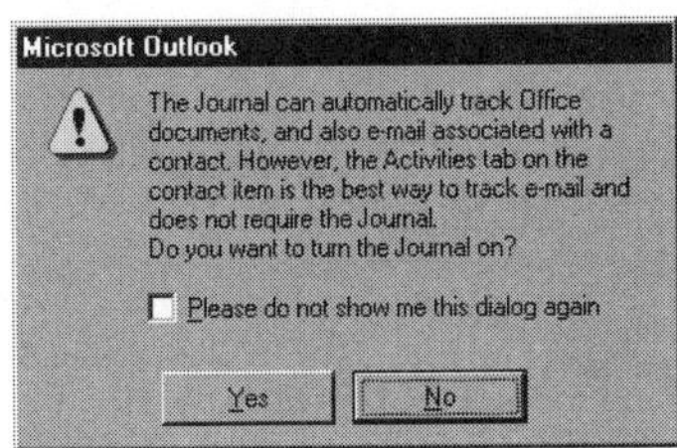

2. Until you are more familiar with the Journal component, you want to manually add journal entries. Click the Please Do Not Show check box and then click No to close the dialog box. Outlook displays the contents of this week's journal in the workspace, like this:

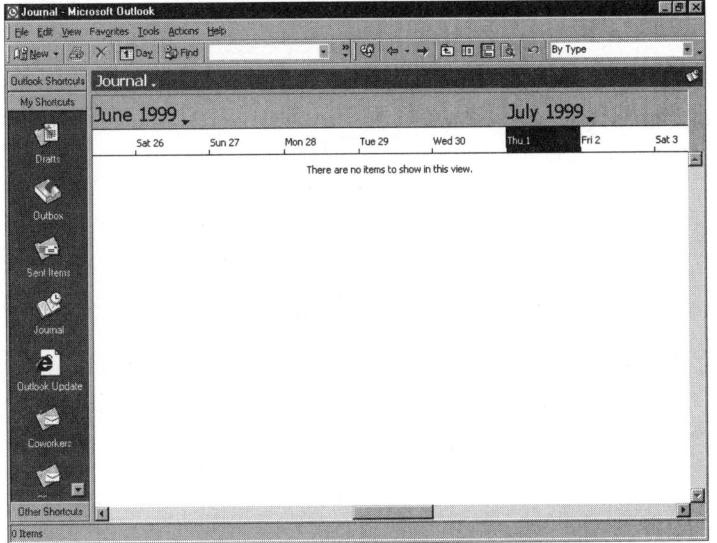

Because Journal is not set to track your activities automatically, the workspace is empty.

Changing Journal tracking defaults

When you are familiar with Journal, you can turn on automatic tracking. Journal can track two types of activities: creating or opening Office files; and sending/receiving e-mail messages, meeting requests/responses, or task requests/responses to and from specified contacts. (You cannot tell Journal to record only e-mail messages for one contact while recording both e-mail messages and task requests for another.) You turn on tracking by choosing Options from the Tools menu, clicking the Journal Options button on the Preferences tab, and selecting what you want Journal to track (see page 133).

Creating Journal Entries

By default, Outlook does not create journal entries for the documents you create or for Outlook items such as e-mail messages, meeting requests, or task requests. In this section, you'll create journal entries for this second type of activity.

Adding an Outlook Item

You can use a couple of different methods to add a journal entry for an Outlook item. We'll show you one way as you create a journal entry for the interview with Dolly Bills:

The New Journal button

1. Click the New Journal button to display a blank Journal Entry window, as shown here:

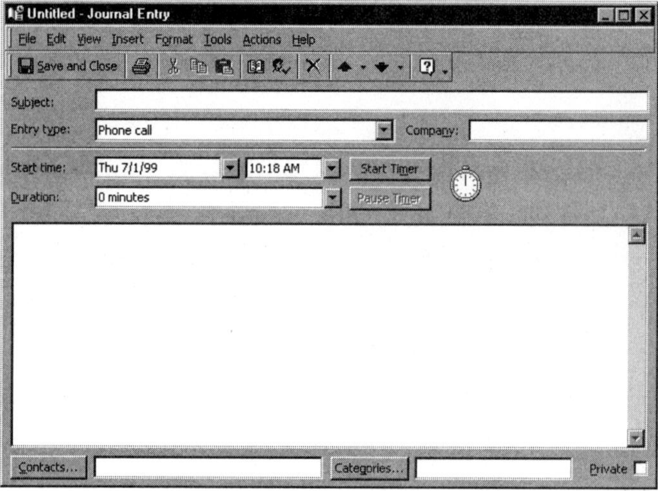

2. Type *Personnel: Dolly Bills* in the Subject edit box, click the arrow to the right of the Entry Type edit box, and select Meeting from the drop-down list.
3. Specify a week prior to today at 4:15 PM as the start time.
4. Next click the arrow to the right of the Duration edit box and select 2 Hours.
5. In the message area, type *Initial interview went well. Bright, articulate, confident; tendency to interrupt. If references check out, invite back for second interview.*

Other ways to add journal entries

If you have the Office shortcut bar installed and want to add a journal entry without opening Outlook, you can click the New Journal Entry button on the Office shortcut bar to quickly open the Journal Entry window. If Outlook is already open, you can choose New and then Journal Entry from the File menu. (You'll have to expand the submenu to see the command.) To use keyboard shortcuts, you can press Ctrl+N from within Journal or press Ctrl+Shift+J from any other Outlook component.

6. Assign the journal entry to the Business category and check the Private check box. Then click Save And Close. Outlook adds a *Meeting* entry type to Journal.

7. Click the plus sign next to the Meeting type and then scroll to the left to display the entry, as shown here:

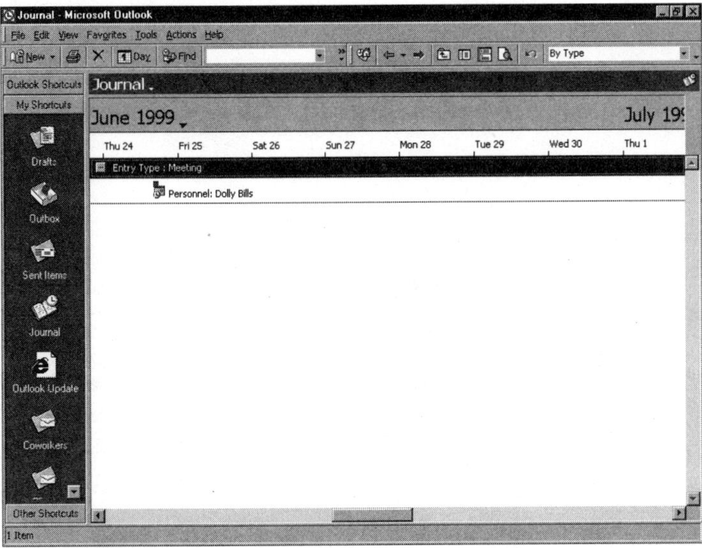

Notice the icon next to the entry name that designates this item as a journal entry.

Now let's try an even easier method for adding journal entries, by adding one for the Boston financial conference that you added to your schedule on page 93:

1. Click the arrow to the right of Journal in the workspace title bar and select Calendar to switch to that component without changing the active group on the Outlook bar.

2. Activate the first day of the Boston financial conference by clicking its date in the date navigator.

3. Point to the conference entry at the top of the day's time slots and drag it to the Journal icon. Outlook displays a partially filled in Journal Entry window, as shown on the next page.

Recording phone calls with Journal

To have Journal record phone calls for a particular contact, you must first set up the call from within Outlook, as described in the tip on page 57. Then in the New Call dialog box, click the Create New Journal Entry check box to record the call. Click the Start Call button to place the call. When you end the call, Outlook displays a Journal Entry window where you can record additional details about the call before clicking Save And Close.

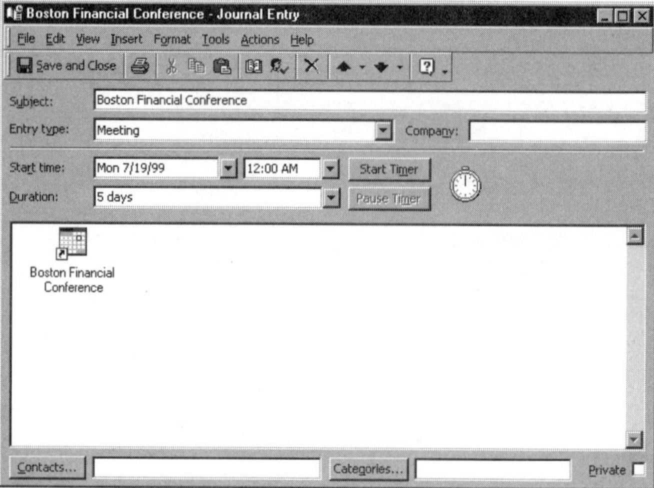

4. Click an insertion point to the right of the appointment's shortcut icon in the message area, press Enter a couple of times, and type *Great conference; very informative; definitely will attend next year.*

5. Click Save And Close.

Moving to a specific date

6. Switch back to Journal and scroll to the right to view the new entry shown below. (You can also click the arrow to the right of the month to display a drop-down calendar and click the appropriate date to move to that section of the timeline.)

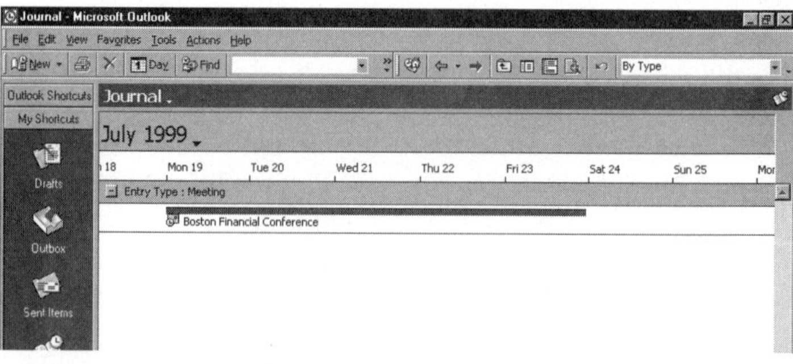

Adding a Contact Activity

In the tip on page 40 in Chapter 2, we briefly discussed how to track activities such as sending e-mail messages to contacts in your contact list. Now let's take a more in-depth look at how this works. Follow the steps on the facing page.

1. Choose Options from the Tools menu. On the Preferences tab, click the Journal Options button to display this dialog box:

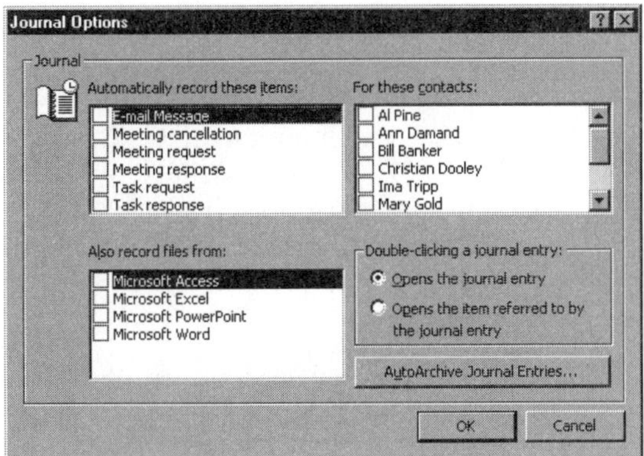

2. Select E-mail Message in the Automatically Record These Items list, click Al Pine in the For These Contacts list, and click OK twice.

3. Click the arrow to the right of the New button on the toolbar and select Mail Message from the drop-down list.

4. In the Message window, type *alp@inthebag.tld* in the To box, type *Reminder* in the Subject box, and type *Just a reminder that there is no meeting this week* in the message area. Then click Send.

5. If necessary, display the Outbox, click the Send/Receive button on the toolbar to send and receive any new messages, and then switch back to Journal.

6. Collapse the Meeting entry type and expand the E-mail Message entry type to see your message, which looks like this:

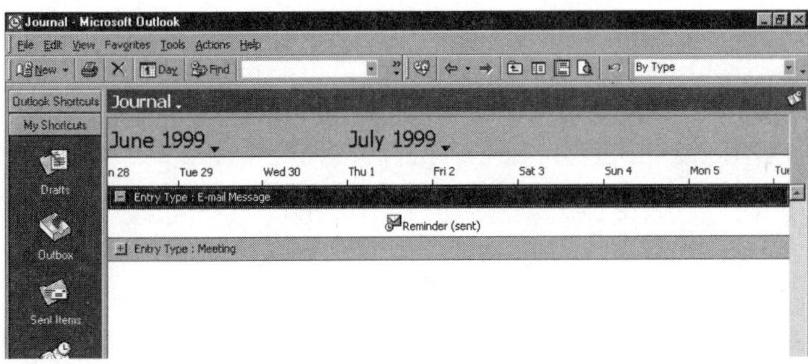

Because the e-mail address for Al Pine is bogus, you will eventually receive a notice that this message is undeliverable. Nevertheless, Outlook has recorded the fact that you sent the message to Mr. Pine.

Now see how Journal and Contacts interact to help you track your activities with the people on your contact list by following these steps:

Checking contact activities

1. Switch to the Contacts component and then double-click the address card for Al Pine.
2. Click the Activities tab. As you can see here, one e-mail message has resulted in three entries that tell you exactly what happened with the message:

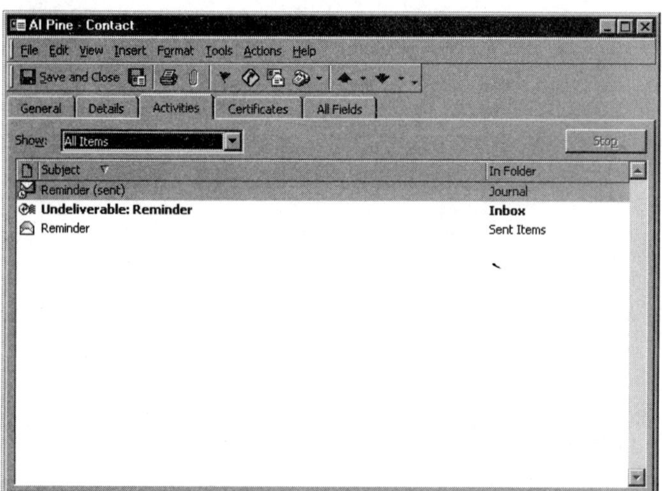

3. Close the Contact window and return to Journal.

Adding a Document

As we mentioned, Outlook can automatically track files created by Office applications. You can also manually add journal entries for a specific document, whether it was created by an Office application or another program. In the steps on the facing page, we use My Computer to show you how to add these journal entries.

1. Click the Other Shortcuts button to display its group of icons on the Outlook bar. Then click the My Computer icon to display its contents in the workspace, as shown here:

The My Computer icon

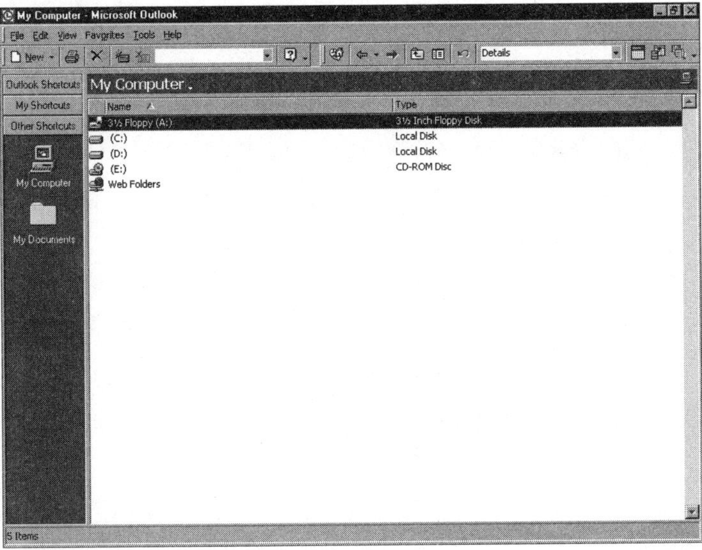

2. Navigate to a file for which you want to add a journal entry and then click it once to select it.

3. Click the My Shortcuts button on the Outlook bar and drag the file selected in the workspace to the Journal icon. When you release the mouse button, Outlook displays a Journal Entry window with most of the information filled in.

4. Add any other information you want for this entry and then click Save And Close.

5. Click the Journal icon to redisplay its contents, and then expand the entry type for the file you selected to see its record.

Viewing your computer's contents in Outlook

When you display the contents of My Computer or My Documents in Outlook's workspace, the files are displayed by default in details view. You can also look at the files in icons view or by type view by changing the Current View setting. If you are working on a network, you can view files on any networked computer to which you have mapped a drive. You can also perform file management tasks such as copying, moving, deleting, and renaming files.

Opening Documents from Journal

Double-clicking a journal entry for a document doesn't open the document in its originating application as you might expect. It opens the Journal Entry window for the document and displays information such as when the document was created, by whom, and the amount of time it was open. Although Journal's main function is to record journal entries for documents and Outlook items, you can also use it to open files that have recorded entries. Let's now try opening a file from Journal:

Opening documents from Journal

1. Right-click the Journal entry you just recorded and then choose Open Item Referred To from the shortcut menu. Outlook instantly opens the item you selected in its originating application.
2. Close the application to return to Outlook.

If you keep Outlook open all the time and frequently open documents from Journal, you can change Outlook's default behavior so that by double-clicking the journal entry, you open the entry's document instead of opening its Journal Entry window. Follow these steps to make this change:

1. Choose Options from the Tools menu and click Journal Options on the Preferences tab.
2. In the Double-Clicking A Journal Entry section, select the Opens The Item option, and click OK twice.
3. Now double-click the document you opened earlier to test the change. Then close the application.
4. To display the document's Journal Entry window instead, right-click the item and then choose Open Journal Entry from the shortcut menu.
5. Close the Journal Entry window.

Starting new documents from Outlook

You can open a new Office document from any of Outlook's components. Click the arrow to the right of the New button on the toolbar and choose Office Document from the expanded drop-down list to display the New Office Document dialog box. Then double-click the icon for the type of document you want to create. (You can also choose New and then Office Document from the File menu.)

Customizing Journal

To wrap up our discussion of the Journal component of Outlook, let's take a look at some of its views so that you can determine which one best suits your needs. First let's take a closer look at the default by type view:

1. So that you can observe journal tracking in action, turn on automatic tracking for Excel and Word. (Choose Options from the Tools menu, click the Journal Options button, click the Microsoft Excel and Microsoft Word check boxes, and click OK twice.)

2. Now create and save two new documents in each of the tracked applications. (Choose New Office Document from the top of the Windows Start menu, double-click the icon you need, save the file, and quit the application.)

3. Back in Journal, display the entries for one application. We chose the Microsoft Word entry type, as shown here:

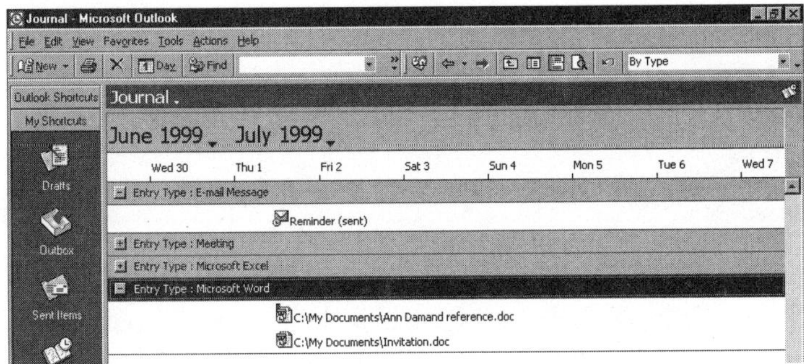

This view shows what you worked on, but it doesn't show how long you spent on the documents. Let's change the view to include times as well as dates:

Changing the Journal view

1. Click the Day button on the toolbar to display a timeline that looks something like the one shown here:

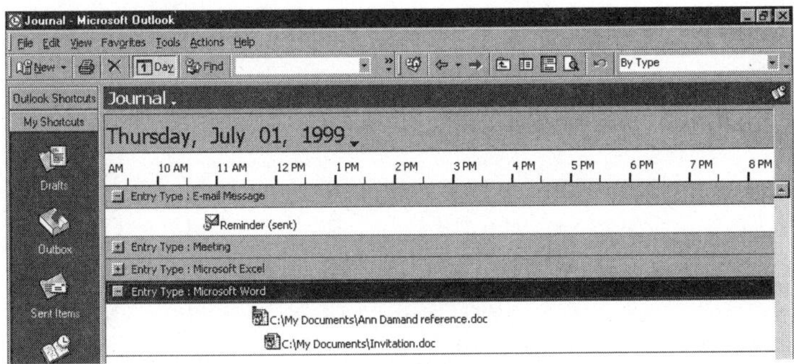

Now you can tell about what time you started the documents, but not when you finished working on them.

2. Click the arrow to the right of the Current View box and select Entry List from the drop-down list. Now all the Journal entries are displayed in table view, as shown on the next page.

Assigning journal entries to categories

You can assign a journal entry to a category by clicking the Categories button in its Journal Entry window. But if several entries belong in the same category, there is a faster way. First hold down the Ctrl key and select all the journal entries you want to assign to a particular category. Then right-click the items you have selected and choose Categories from the shortcut menu. In the Categories dialog box, click the appropriate category and then click OK.

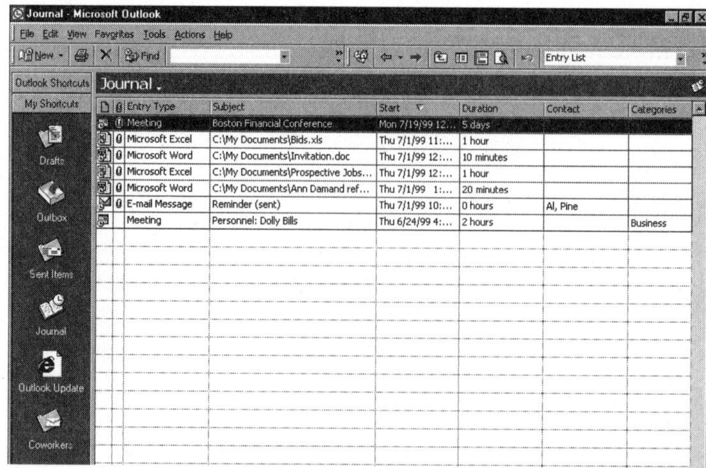

In this view you see Icon, Attachment, Entry Type, Subject, Start, Duration, Contact, and Categories columns. The amount of time you spent on each document is indicated in the Duration column. As with the other Outlook views, this view can be customized to show only the information you need. (See page 21 for more information.) We'll leave you to experiment with customization on your own.

3. Select By Type from the Current View drop-down list and then click the Week button on the Standard toolbar to return to the default view. (See the adjacent tip for information about other Journal views.)

> **Other Journal views**
>
> Outlook offers four other predefined Journal views: by contact, by category, last seven days, and phone calls. The by contact and by category views are timeline views with grouping boxes for either contact names or categories. The last seven days view is a table view that displays entries up to seven days old. The phone calls view is another table view that displays only phone calls made through Outlook. Remember, you can modify these views to suit your tastes, and you can create completely new ones.

Archiving Outlook Files

As promised, we are going to end this chapter with a discussion of archiving Outlook files. The more you use Outlook, the more its files will grow. (The size of the files can increase pretty quickly if you have certain options selected; see the tip on the facing page.) If you archive old Outlook files, you can keep the current files at a reasonable size. You can always retrieve the archived files if you need to look up old information (see the tip on page 140). You can have Outlook automatically archive your files at specified intervals, or you can do the archiving manually. Let's look at both methods:

1. Click the Folder List button on the Advanced toolbar to display the folders for the Outlook components.

2. Right-click the Calendar folder and choose Properties from the shortcut menu. Then click the AutoArchive tab of the Calendar Properties dialog box to display these options:

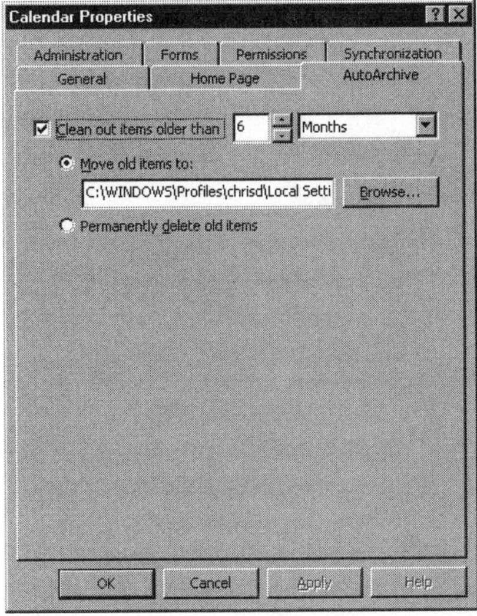

3. Click an insertion point in the Move Old Items To edit box and press End to move to the end of the current entry. As you can see, old Calendar items will be moved to a file called archive.pst. To save the archive file in another location, either enter the path in the Move Old Items To edit box or use the Browse button. (You can select the Permanently Delete Old Items option to delete the items instead of archiving them.)
4. Check that the Clean Out Items Older Than check box is selected and then set the time to 3 months (or select the time interval you think is most appropriate for your work).
5. Click OK to apply the new setting.
6. Repeat this procedure for all the other Outlook folders except Contacts, which contains only active items. (Outlook may not automatically select the Clean Out Items check box for some folders, so you may need to select it first.)
7. If necessary, select Journal in the folder list and then click the list's Close button.

Maintaining a small Outlook file

To maintain a small Outlook file, you can take the following preventative measures, some of which have already been mentioned in this book:

- Empty the Deleted Items folder on a regular basis. (You can tell Outlook to automatically empty this folder every time you exit Outlook by choosing Options from the Tools menu, clicking the Other tab, and then clicking the Empty The Deleted Items Folder Upon Exiting check box.)
- Turn off the option to save copies of your sent messages (see the tip on page 75).
- Record only necessary journal entries. If you find you don't use the feature at all, don't record any journal entries.
- Archive your files frequently so that Outlook can get rid of old files.
- Compact your personal folder files. Choose Services from the Tools menu, select Microsoft Exchange Server on the Services tab, and then click the Properties button. Click the Advanced tab and then click the Offline Folder File Settings button. Finally, click the Compact Now button. When Outlook is finished compacting the files, click OK three times to close all of the dialog boxes.

Now you need to verify that the AutoArchive feature is activated. Follow these steps:

Setting AutoArchive options

1. Choose Options from the Tools menu, click the Other tab, and click the AutoArchive button to display these options:

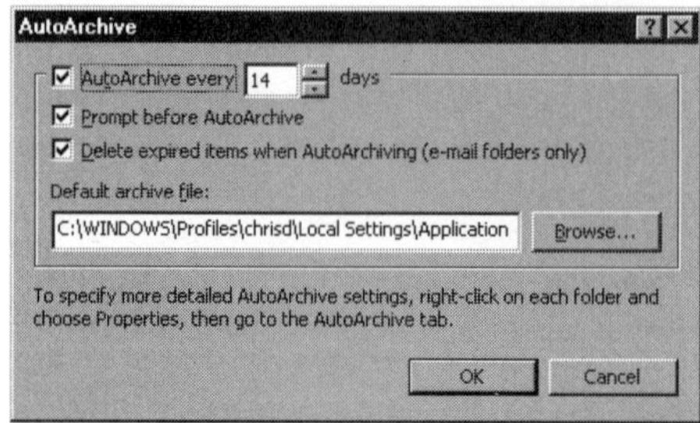

Here you can specify how often you want archiving to occur, whether you want to be prompted, and whether expired e-mail messages should be sent to the Deleted Items folder. If you select the Prompt Before AutoArchive check box, Outlook displays a message box when it is ready to begin archiving. If you then click No to delay archiving, Outlook reminds you about archiving every time you open the program until you complete the process.

2. If you want, change any settings to meet your particular needs and then click OK twice.

Restoring an archived file

You can use one of two methods to restore archived Outlook files. If you need the files only temporarily, open them in a separate Archive Folders folder. Choose Open from the File menu, choose Personal Folders File (.pst), navigate to the archive file you want to open, and click OK in the Open Personal Folders dialog box. Outlook then displays the contents of Archive Folders in the workspace. You can open the Folder List as usual to get to the information you need. When you have finished using the archived files, right-click the appropriate Archive Folders file and choose Close "Archive Folders" from the shortcut menu. The second method requires you to import the archived file into your Personal Folders file. (If necessary, choose New and then Personal Folders File (.pst) from the File menu. Navigate to the Outlook folder in the Create Personal Folders dialog box and click Create. Then click OK to accept the default in the Create Microsoft Personal Folders dialog box.) Choose Import And Export from the File menu, select Import From Another Program Or File, and then click Next. Select Personal Folder File (.pst) as the file type and click Next. Select the file you want to import by using the Browse button, and select the duplicates option you want in the Options section. Then click Next. Select the folder and any subfolders you want to import, check that Personal Folders is selected in the Import Items Into The Same Folder In box, and click Finish. Outlook imports the files in the designated locations. You then open the Folder List to access the information.

Here are the steps for archiving files manually:

Archiving files manually

1. Choose Archive from the expanded File menu to display the dialog box shown here:

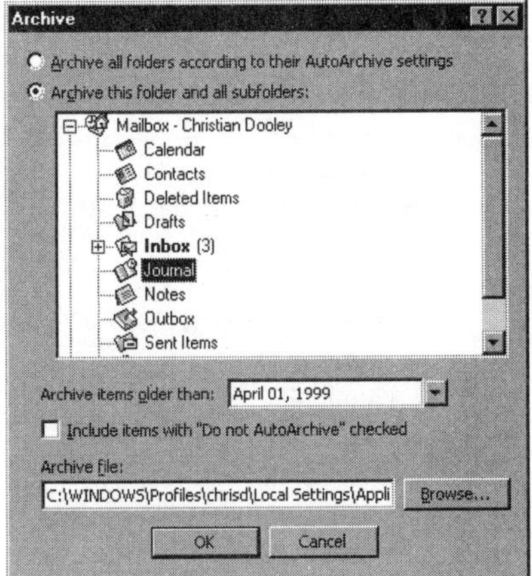

You can use the two options at the top of the dialog box to either archive according to the settings specified in each component's Properties dialog box, or to select a specific folder (or all of them if you select your Mailbox folder) and archive all items older than a certain date. To specify the date, click the arrow to the right of the Archive Items Older Than edit box and select a date in the date navigator.

2. You aren't actually going to archive right now, so click Cancel to close the dialog box.

As you have seen, by faithfully using Outlook's Journal, you can keep better track of your time. And by allowing the program's archiving features to take care of old items, you can keep your Outlook files to a manageable size.

Congratulations! You have completed your *Quick Course in Microsoft Outlook 2000*. By now, you should feel comfortable with all the components of this program. With the basics you have learned in this book, together with the Help feature, you should have no trouble creating any Outlook item and keeping items organized the way you want.

Index

A

active appointments view 97
active tasks view 120
activities
  tracking for contacts 40, 132
  viewing 134
address books 67
  Contacts 36, 67
  creating labels/form letters from 56
  Global Address List 56, 67
  and mail merge 56
  Outlook 56
address cards 37
  adding personal information 40
  assigning to categories 39, 43
  creating 37, 42
  deleting 41
  editing 39
  organizing 42
  saving 39
address cards view 43
addresses, displaying maps of 58
addressing e-mail messages 64
  using contacts list 67
  using distribution lists 68
Advanced toolbar 9, 36
aligning controls/labels on contact form 50
Align Left button 50
Align/Left command 50
anniversaries, entering for contacts 41
Answer Wizard 32
appointments. *See also* events
  allocating more time for 94
  attaching files to 90
  canceling 95
  converting to tasks 113
  creating from e-mail messages 88
  custom time slots 87
  editing 93
  finding 96
  locations for 88
  moving among 93
  private 89
  recurring 90
    canceling 96
    editing 95
  reminders 88, 90
  rescheduling 93
  scheduling 87
  status of 88
Archive command 141
archived files, restoring 140
archiving files 138
assignment view 120
Assign Task button 122
attaching
  files to appointments 90
  notes to other items 18
attachments to e-mail messages 71, 72
  files 68
  reading 71
  saving 74
AutoArchive 139
AutoCreate 113
AutoPick button 100
AutoPreview button 10

B

Best Fit command (shortcut menu) 46
birthdays, entering for contacts 41
buttons
  adding/removing from toolbar 11
  displaying/hiding 10
  toolbar 8
by category view 20, 45, 119, 138
by color view 20
by contact view 138
by conversation topic view 76
by person responsible view 120
by type view 136

C

Calendar 5, 86
  adding
    holidays 94
    time zones 104
  changing time interval 103
  customizing 103
  jumping to today 89
  printing schedules 106
  reminders in 88, 90
Calendar icon 86
Call Contact command 57
canceling
  appointments 95
    recurring 96
  meetings 102
Cancel Meeting command 102
categories
  assigning
    address cards to 39, 43
    notes to 15
  creating 43
  Master Category List 43
Categories command 15
Categorize command (shortcut menu) 118, 137
categorizing
  contacts 39, 43
  journal entries 131, 137
  tasks 113, 118
certificates 40
Check For New Mail command 133
closing notes 13
Color command 14
color of notes, changing 14
columns, sizing 46
  in views 20
commands, menu 8
compacting folders 139
completed tasks 115, 127
completed tasks view 120
contacts
  adding
    birthdays/anniversaries 41
    e-mail addresses to list 67
    to list 37, 42
    from other components 38
    personal information 40
  address cards. *See* address cards
  categorizing 39, 43
  e-mail/Web page addresses 38
  finding in Outlook Today 127
  flagging for follow-up 45
  forms. *See* forms, contact

importing/exporting 37
letter tabs 44
organizing 42
phoning 57
printing list of 58
sending e-mail messages to 68
sorting 45
switching views 43
tracking 40, 129, 132
viewing activities in Journal 134
writing letters with 55

Contacts 5, 36
Contacts icon 36, 134
controls on contact forms 50
Control Toolbox button 52
converting notes to tasks 17
copying
- tasks 115
- views 23, 47

courtesy copies of e-mail messages 65
Create Microsoft Outlook Task button 111
Create Shortcut Wizard 6
Current View box 10, 43, 47, 76, 107
Current View/By Conversation Topic command 76
Current View command 19, 44
Current View/Customize Current View command 21, 77
Current View/Define Views command 22, 25, 47
custom
- appointment time slots 87
- contact forms 48
- views 21, 22, 45
  - adding/removing fields 45, 46
  - deleting 25
  - saving 47
  - sizing columns 46

Customize Current View command (shortcut menu) 78
customizing
- Calendar 103
- Journal 136
- Outlook bar 27

D

date navigator 87
Day button 107, 137
day view 103
default
- contact forms 55
- journal entries 132
- tasks 117

delegating tasks 120
Delete button 19, 42, 75, 95, 116
Deleted Items folder 75, 116
- emptying 139
- retrieving items from 19

Deleted Items icon 75
deleting
- address cards 41
- appointments 95
  - recurring 96
- contact forms 55
- custom views 25
- e-mail messages 74
  - when quitting 75
- notes 18
- tasks 116
- undoing 19, 96

design view 48
desktop, moving notes to 16
detailed address cards view 43
detailed list view 118
dialing phone numbers 57
digital IDs 40
Display This Page command 53
distribution lists 68
docking toolbars 9
documents
- linking to tasks 111
- opening from Journal 136
- starting new from Outlook 136
- tracking in Journal 134

Drafts folder 63
due dates, assigning to tasks 111, 113, 115

E

editing
- address cards 39
- appointments 93
  - recurring 95
- contact forms 54
- contacts 39
- meeting requests 101
- notes 14
- redoing 19
- tasks 114
- undoing 19

e-mail 4, 7, 62
- addresses
  - adding to contact list 67
  - for contacts 38
- internal vs. Internet 62
- Internet, setting up 62
- messages 64
  - addressing 64, 67
  - attachments 68, 70, 74
  - certificates 40
  - converting to tasks 113
  - courtesy copies 65
  - creating appointments from 88
  - creating message folders 78
  - deleting 74, 75
  - digital IDs 40
  - distribution lists 68
  - drafts 63
  - eliminating original in replies 73
  - encrypting 40, 65
  - filtering 77, 78
  - flagging 71
  - forwarding 73
  - header symbols 70
  - marking 71
  - moving 80
  - notifying of receipt 65
  - not saving in Sent Items 75
  - organizing 75, 80
  - previewing 10, 71
  - priority, setting 65
  - reading 71
  - recalling 76
  - replying to 72
  - retrieving 70, 74
  - saving 74
  - saving attachments 74
  - security 40, 65
  - selecting 75, 80
  - sending 64, 66, 68, 69, 73, 74
  - signatures 66
  - tracking 129

viewing 76
voting buttons, adding 66
writing 64, 67, 68
Empty Deleted Items Folder command 75
events
recurring 93
scheduling 91
Exchange 5, 63
Exit command 33
exporting contacts 37

F

Field Chooser 46, 48
fields 45
adding to contact form 49
adding to/removing from views 24, 45, 46
grouping by 22
moving in views 24
files
archived, restoring 140
archiving 138
attaching
to appointments 90
to e-mail messages 68
managing with My Computer 135
moving to another Outlook group 28
filling in contact forms 53
filtering e-mail messages 77, 78
filters 77
Find button 96
finding
appointments 96
contacts 127
Flag For Follow Up command (shortcut menu) 71
flagging
contacts for follow-up 45
e-mail messages 71
floating toolbars 9
Folder button 138
folder list
displaying 26, 79
hiding 80
keeping open 27
Folder List button 79
Folder List command 27, 79
Folder/New Folder command 78
folders
compacting 139
creating in Outlook 28
creating Outlook bar shortcuts for 28
displaying 138
for e-mail messages 78
moving to another Outlook group 28
organizing 27
form letters (Word), creating from address books 56
forms, contact
adding fields 49
aligning controls/labels 50
custom 48
deleting 55
editing 54
filling in 53
hiding pages 53
labels/controls 50
naming 53
opening 49, 55
saving 53
selecting 54
setting default 55
sizing controls/labels 51
Forms/Design This Form command 48, 49
Forward As Vcard command 66
Forward button 73
forwarding e-mail messages 73

G

Global Address List 56, 67
Go To Today button 89
gridlines in views, changing 24
Group By Box command (shortcut menu) 22
Group By This Field command (shortcut menu) 22
grouping items/notes 21
groups on Outlook bar 11, 29

H

handles
move 9
selection 50
headers, symbols 70
help 30
Web 32
hidden commands, displaying 8
Hide Office Assistant command 31
Hide Outlook Bar command 26
hiding
contact form pages 53
Outlook bar 26
holidays, adding/removing 94
Horizontal Spacing command 51

I

icons
on Outlook bar
moving 29
sizing 12
small/large views 19
Import And Export command 37, 140
importing contacts 37
Inbox 4, 7, 63. *See also* e-mail, messages
Inbox icon 64
Insert File button 68, 90
internal e-mail 63
Internet Connection Wizard 62
Internet e-mail 63
Internet service providers (ISPs) 63
Item command 18

J

Journal 5, 40, 128
journal entries
categorizing 131, 137
contact activities 132
creating 130
defaults, changing 129
documents 134
Outlook items 130
phone calls 131
viewing 129
Journal icon 129
junk e-mail, filtering 78

L

labels
on contact forms 50
in Word, creating from address books 56
Large Icons button 19
Large icons command 12
large icons view 19
last seven days view 21, 138

letters
form, creating from address books 56
writing from Contacts 55
letter tabs (contact list) 44
Letter Wizard 55
linking tasks and documents 111
List button 19
lists
contact 36
distribution (e-mail) 68
folder 26, 79
list, to-do. *See* to-do list
list view 19

M

mail merge (Word) and Outlook Address Book 56
Make Same Width button 52
maps of addresses, displaying 58
Mark Complete button 116
marking e-mail messages 71
Master Category List 43
meetings
canceling 102
online 99
planning 98
requests 100
menu bar 8
menus 8
messages view 76
Microsoft Exchange 5, 63
Microsoft NetMeeting 98
Microsoft Office 2000 6, 128
Microsoft Outlook Help button 30
Microsoft Outlook Help command 31
Microsoft Outlook icon 6
Microsoft Word 55
minimizing
notes 17
Outlook 16
modes, corporate vs. Internet support 6
Month button 106
month view 105
More Buttons button 10
move handle 9
moving
appointments 93
among components 12, 26
controls/labels on contact forms 51
e-mail messages 80
fields in views 24
folders/files to another group 28
icons on Outlook bar 29
notes to desktop 16
toolbars 9
My Computer
displaying in Outlook 28
within Outlook 135
My Computer icon 135

N

naming contact forms 53
NetMeeting 98
New All Day Event command 93
New/Appointment command 87
New Appointment command (shortcut menu) 87
New button 87, 111
New Contact button 37, 42, 48
New/Contact command 38
New Journal button 130
New Journal Entry button (Office shortcut bar) 130
New/Journal Entry command 130
New Letter To Contact command 55
New Mail Message button 64, 67, 68
New Meeting Request command 100
New Message To Contact command 133
New Message To Contact command (shortcut menu) 68
New Note button 13
New/Note command 13
New/Personal Folders File command 140
New Recurring Appointment command 90
New Recurring Meeting command 101
New Task button 112, 114
New Tasks Request command 120
Next Folder command 27
next seven days view 120
note boxes 13
sizing 15
notes
attaching to other items 18
categorizing 15
closing 13
color of, changing 14
converting to tasks 17
creating 13
defaults, changing 15
deleting 18
editing 14
grouping/sorting 21
minimizing on taskbar 17
moving to desktop 16
saving 14
selecting 14, 17
sorting by category 15, 22
Notes 5, 12
Notes icon 12
notes list view 19

O

Office Assistant 6, 30
offline, working 63
online meetings 99
opening
address cards 42
contact forms 54, 55
documents from Journal 136
Open Item Referred To command (shortcut menu) 136
Open Special Folder/Personal Folders File command 140
Organize button 27
organizing
contacts 42
e-mail messages 75
by filtering 77
with Rules Wizard 80
folders 27
tasks 117
Outbox 66, 68
sending e-mail messages from 70, 74
Outbox icon 66
outgoing e-mail messages
not saving in Sent Items 75
options 65

Outlook
- Address Book 56
- minimizing 16
- moving among components 12, 26
- quitting 33
- starting 6
- starting component, changing 6, 127
- starting new documents from 136
- templates 74

Outlook 2000 Startup Wizard 6
Outlook bar 11
- adding/removing groups 29
- creating shortcuts on 28
- customizing 27
- displaying small/large icons 12
- groups 11
- moving icons on 29
- sizing 26
- turning on/off 26, 27, 80

Outlook Bar command 80
Outlook Today 4, 126
- finding contacts 127

Outlook Today icon 126
overdue tasks view 120
ownership of tasks 121

P

pages in contact forms 53
personal information, adding to address cards 40
phone calls, tracking 131
phone calls view 138
phone list view 44
phone numbers, dialing 57
Plan A Meeting command 98
planning meetings 98
previewing e-mail messages 10, 71
Previous Folder command 27
Print button 58, 106
Print command 106
printing
- contacts 58
- schedules 106

priority
- of messages 65
- of tasks, setting 112, 113, 115

private appointments 89
Publish Form button 53
push pin icon 27

Q

quitting Outlook 33

R

reading e-mail messages 71
reassigning tasks 122
recalling e-mail messages 76
receipt of e-mail messages, notifying 65
records 45
Recurrence button 96
recurring
- appointments 90
  - canceling 96
  - editing 95
- events 93
- meetings 101
- tasks 114

Redo Edit command 19
reminders
- in Calendar 88, 90
- in Tasks 113, 114

Remove This Column command (shortcut menu) 45
removing
- fields from views 24, 45
- filters 78
- flags 45

Rename Group command (shortcut menu) 29
Rename Page command 53
renaming groups 29
Reply button 72
replying to e-mail messages 72
- eliminating original e-mail message 73

Reply To All button 72
rescheduling appointments 93
responding
- to meeting requests 102
- to task requests 122

restoring
- archived files 140
- views 47

retrieving e-mail messages 70, 74
Rules Wizard 80
- updating manually 83

Rules Wizard button 80
Run This Form command 54

S

Save And Close button 39
Save And New button 39
Save As command 14
Save Attachments command 74
saving
- address cards 39
- attachments to e-mail messages 74
- contact forms 53
- custom views 47
- e-mail messages 74
- notes 14

schedules, printing 106
scheduling
- appointments 87
- events 91
- tasks 110

ScreenTips 9, 30
searching for help 30
security, e-mail 40, 65
Select All command 75
selecting
- contact forms 54
- e-mail messages 80
  - all 75
- notes 14, 17

selection handles 50
Send And Receive button 70, 74
Send And Receive command 70
Send button 66, 68, 69, 73, 101
sending
- e-mail messages 64, 66, 68, 69, 73, 74
- meeting requests 100
- task requests 120

Send Update button 102
Sent Items folder 74
- turning off automatic save 75

Sent Items icon 75
Services command 139
shortcuts, creating on Outlook bar 28
Signature button 66
signatures 66
simple list view 111
Size To Fit command 51

sizing
  columns 46
    in views 20
  controls/labels on contact form 51
  note boxes 15
  Outlook bar 26
  workspace 26
Small Icons button 19
Small Icons command 12
small icons view 19
Snap To Grid button 51
sorting
  contacts 45
  notes 15, 21
  tasks 117
Standard toolbar 8
starting
  component, changing 6, 127
  document from Outlook 136
  Outlook 6
status bar 7
  turning on/off 26
Status Bar command 26
status
  of appointments 88
  of tasks 113, 115
    in Outlook Today 127
switching views 19, 43, 76, 103, 105, 111, 118

T

task list. *See* to-do list
TaskPad 87
tasks
  adding
    with AutoCreate 113
    to to-do list 110, 112
  assigning due date 111, 113, 115
  categorizing 113, 118
  changing defaults 117
  completed 115, 127
  converting 113
    from appointments 113
    from e-mail messages 113
    from notes 17
  copying 115
  creating 114
  delegating 120
  deleting 116
  editing 114
  linking to documents 111
  organizing 117
  ownership 121
  priority, setting 112, 113, 115
  reassigning 122
  recurring 114
  reminders 113, 114
  requests
    responding to 122
    sending 120
  scheduling 110
  sorting 117
  status, setting 113, 115
    in Outlook Today 127
Tasks 5, 110
Tasks icon 17, 110
task timeline view 120
templates, Outlook 74
time management 86
time slots 87
  changing interval 103
  custom 87
time zones, adding 104
title bar 7
to-do list 5, 110
  adding tasks 110, 112, 113
toolbar row 9
toolbars
  adding/removing buttons 11
  Advanced 9, 36
  displaying more/fewer buttons 10
  docking/floating/moving 9
  Standard 8
  turning on/off 9, 11, 36
toolbox 52
tracking
  contacts 40, 129, 132
  documents in Journal 134
  phone calls 131

U

undeleting items 19
Undo button 19
Undo Delete command 19, 96
undoing editing 19
unread messages view 76
updating meeting requests 102

V

Vertical Spacing command 51
viewing
  contact activities 134
  e-mail messages 76
  journal entries 129
views
  active appointments 97
  active tasks 120
  address cards 43
  assignment 120
  by category 20, 45, 119, 138
  by color 20
  by contact 138
  by conversation topic 76
  by person responsible 120
  by type 136
  completed tasks 120
  copying 23, 47
  custom 21, 22, 45
    adding/removing fields 45, 46
    deleting 25
    saving 47
    sizing columns 46
  day 103
  design 48
  detailed address cards 43
  detailed list 118
  fields in 24
  gridlines in, changing 24
  large icons 19
  last seven days 21, 138
  list 19
  messages 76
  month 105
  next seven days 120
  notes list 19
  overdue tasks 120
  phone calls 138
  phone list 44
  restoring 47
  simple list 111
  sizing columns in 20
  small icons 19
  switching 19, 43, 76, 103, 105, 111, 118
  task timeline 120
  unread messages 76
  week 105
  work week 105

virtual business cards
  (vcards) 66
voting buttons, adding to e-mail
  messages 66

W

Web, help on 32
Web page addresses in
  Contacts 38
Week button 105, 138
weekdays, adjusting 91
week view 105
wizards
  Answer 32
  Create Shortcut 6
  Internet Connection 62
  Letter 55
  Outlook 2000 Startup 6
  Rules 80
Word 55
workday, changing 89
working offline 63
workspace 12
  sizing 26
workweek, changing 89
work week view 105
writing
  e-mail messages 64, 67, 69
  letters from Contacts 55

See clearly—now!

Here's the remarkable, *visual* way to quickly find answers about the powerfully integrated features of the Microsoft® Office 2000 applications. Microsoft Press AT A GLANCE books let you focus on particular tasks and show you, with clear, numbered steps, the easiest way to get them done right now. Put Office 2000 to work today, with AT A GLANCE learning solutions, made by Microsoft.

- MICROSOFT OFFICE 2000 PROFESSIONAL AT A GLANCE
- MICROSOFT WORD 2000 AT A GLANCE
- MICROSOFT EXCEL 2000 AT A GLANCE
- MICROSOFT POWERPOINT® 2000 AT A GLANCE
- MICROSOFT ACCESS 2000 AT A GLANCE
- MICROSOFT FRONTPAGE® 2000 AT A GLANCE
- MICROSOFT PUBLISHER 2000 AT A GLANCE
- MICROSOFT OFFICE 2000 SMALL BUSINESS AT A GLANCE
- MICROSOFT PHOTODRAW® 2000 AT A GLANCE
- MICROSOFT INTERNET EXPLORER 5 AT A GLANCE
- MICROSOFT OUTLOOK® 2000 AT A GLANCE

Microsoft Press products are available worldwide wherever quality computer books are sold. For more information, contact your book or computer retailer, software reseller, or local Microsoft Sales Office, or visit our Web site at mspress.microsoft.com. To locate your nearest source for Microsoft Press products, or to order directly, call 1-800-MSPRESS in the U.S. (in Canada, call 1-800-268-2222).

Prices and availability dates are subject to change.

mspress.microsoft.com